# KNOWLEDGE

# AND

# WISDOM

# Meaningful Life

Nges Elmer Kimbi

Copyright © 2020 Nges Elmer Kimbi



ISBN:9798605162995

# INTRODUCTION

*Ours is a world of nuclear giants and ethical infants. We know more about war than we know about peace, more about killing than we know about living. We have grasped the mystery of the atom and rejected the Sermon on the Mount.*          **(Omar N. Bradley)**

Yes! Despite all the technological tools in our age, **life** appears to have lost meaning and value. We seem to have abandoned our core values. We fuss and fret over **life** and its enjoyments; take so much care to perpetuate our good names and fortune; and weigh every event as a means of self-aggrandizement.

These, notwithstanding, we have met with emptiness, dejection and destitution. We have lost faith in our government, in ourselves, and even in God. We have resigned in self-pity and have sunk into frustration and desperation. We have questioned the rationale for living. What are we here for?

Absolutely, we need doctors, lawyers, engineers, politicians, teachers, businessmen, et cetera, to keep *life* going.

But what are we keeping *life* going for when every day; we are witnesses to natural and man-triggered devastations which consume millions of lives within moments? Earthquakes, tsunamis, floods, hurricanes, tornados, volcanic eruptions, landslides, bombings, plane crashes, fatal accidents, etc. have become ordinary events. In view of these calamities, which have become ordinary events, is ***life meaningful?*** What is *life* all about?

This book throws light on *life*. *Life* is more than talent, genius, education, position, and wealth. The book is an embodiment of a multiplicity of varying selected beautiful quotations which deal on the concept of *life* in some of its endless ramifications. These quotations have been collected, leisurely, from many books and volumes within the past years. Effort has been made to group these quotations in chapters under suitable themes. Effort has also been made to arrange them to flow in a prose-like order, gradually and smoothly leading the reader into the main theme of the chapter. The quotations are intended to provide a deep insight into the various themes relation to *life* and give the reader not only an optimistic but a holistic and realistic view of *life*.

These quotations, of which many are like short eloquent speeches loaded with meaning, constitute an answer to some of *life* searching questions. They are thoughts, ideas, and beliefs of great men and women, past and present. The wisdom in them is known to have energized and positively transformed the lives of our predecessors in bygone days. King Solomon in his book of Proverbs is succinct:

*Happy is anyone who becomes wise - who comes to have understanding. ... Wisdom is more valuable than jewels; nothing you could want can compare with it. Wisdom offers you long life, as well as wealth and honour. Wisdom can make your **life** pleasant and lead you safely through it. ... My child, hold on to your wisdom and insight. Never let them get away from you. ... You can go safely on your way and never even stumble. You will not be afraid when you go to bed, and you will sleep soundly through the night.* **(Prov. 3:13, 15-17, 21, 23-24)**

It is hoped that we, of today who are still enjoying **life** on earth, cannot be indifferent to this time-tested wisdom. It is also hoped that from the quotations, the reader may accept and appreciate the fact that ***LIFE IS MEANINGFUL.***

In a way, we may be consoled and guaranteed that *life* is worth living. No matter your present status in *life*, there is no doubt that some of the quotations will apply directly to you and even impact your *life.* It can be lovely and joyous finding one's own ideas and thoughts beautifully crafted and authoritatively presented by much wiser persons.

It is to be hoped that this compressed book will not only be for the general and casual reader, but may serve as resource material to, among others, speakers, preachers, teachers and writers.

For the books and volumes, I consulted, care has been taken to give credit wherever possible. If for any reason an omission has occurred anywhere, or I have failed to acknowledge the correct source of any material, I sincerely apologize for that.

Quotations which are anonymous or whose authors are unknown are referenced as **(***)**. The font size of the text has been made large to ease reading, even to those with weak eyesight.

*I gather the flowers by the way side, by small streams and near the rivers, and only the strings with which I bind them together are my own.*
                                                    **(Montaigne, 1533-92)**

# CONTENTS

# DEDICATION

To lovers of knowledge and wisdom in all its forms

# CHAPTER ONE
## LIFE IS *"A STRUGGLE"*.

*T*here has never been a ***meaningful life*** built on   easy street.   *(John Paul Warren)*

2. **Life** is a hard fight, a struggle, a wrestling with the principle of evil, hand to hand, foot to foot. Every inch of the way is disputed. The night is given us to take breath, to pray, to drink at the fountain of power. The day, to use the strength to which has

been given us, to go forth to work with it till the evening. **(Florence Nightingale)**

3. *S*truggle, hard struggle, is the law of progress. Yes, struggle we must, both internal as well as with others. There must be a struggle between truth and untruth, between vice and virtue, between honesty and dishonesty, between expediency and righteousness, between indolence and energy, between enterprise and spirit of lethargy and between time-seeing selfishness and noble disinterestedness. Without this struggle no nation can ever aspire to be great and influential.

**(Lala Lajpat Rai)**

4. **Life** affords no higher pleasure than that of **surmounting** difficulties, passing from one step of success to another, forming new wishes and seeing them gratified. **(Dr. Samuel Johnson)**

5. **Be** strong! We are not here to play, to dream, to drift; we have hard work to do; and loads to lift; shun not the struggle–face it; it's God's gift.

**(Malthie V. Babcock)**

6. *T*here are three ways that prepare us for **life's** trials. One is the Spartan way that says, "I have strength within me to do it, I am the captain of my soul. With the courage and will that is mine; I will be master when the struggle comes." Another way is in the spirit of Socrates, who affirmed that we have minds, reason and judgment to evaluate and help us to cope with the enigmas and struggles of **life**. The Christian way is the third approach. It doesn't

exclude the first two but it adds, "You don't begin with yourself, your will, or your reason. You begin with God, who is the beginning and the end. When your strength grows weak and your reason fails you, faith in the creator gives you the power to overcome all things." **(L. R. Dttzen)**

7. **E**verybody has problems. No **life** is problem-free.
**(Robert Schuller)**

8. **N**obody's **life** is smooth and easy. Everybody has ups and downs. We've got to expect that and, since we should expect it, we should be ready for it, prepared for it. Then, when it happens, we accept it naturally, as a challenge, as a measure of the stuff of which we are made. Indeed, we may even be eager to try ourselves out, to discover how capable we really are. **(Louis Bisch)**

9. **A life** merely of pleasure, or chiefly of pleasure, is always a poor and worthless **life**.
**(Theodore W. Parker)**

10. **Life** on earth is like a battle against evil-forces. You must fight on without retreat. **(***)**

11. **I**f you think you are beaten, you are.
If you think you dare not, you don't.
If you like to win, but you think you can't,
It is almost certain you won't.
If you think you will lose, you are lost,
For out of the world we find,
Success begins with a fellow's will-
It's all in the state of mind.

If you think you are outclassed, you are,
You've got to think high to rise,

You've got to be sure of yourself before you can ever win a prize. *Life's* battles don't always go to the stronger or faster man, but soon or late the man who wins is the man **WHO THINKS HE CAN.**                    *(Napoleon Hill)*

12. *Life*, from birth to death, is like a meandering river flowing into an ocean from its source. In the course of its lonely journey, the river, like a man, is faced with lots of problems which must be surmounted if the journey must continue.     *(***)*

13. *E*very mountain has a peak. Every valley has its lowest point. Every cloud has its silver lining. *Life* has its ups and downs, its peaks and valleys. No one is up all the time. Problems do end. Storms always give way to calms.     *(***)*

14. *M*en are by nature neither kings nor grandees, nor courtiers, no millionaires; all are born naked and poor; all are subject to the miseries o*f life*, to chagrins, evils, needs, and sorrows of every sort, and finally all are condemned to death.
                    *(Jean Jacques Rousseau)*

15. *T*he man who cannot live with doubts is a troubled person. For to have all doubts settled is to have no mental pursuits taking place. And such a man, while of little trouble to himself, is also of little help to others. Doubts can be valuable if they force a man to search deeper and longer for

answers. For to pursue the doubts is to come upon some exciting beliefs and truths.     *(C. Neil Strait)*

16. *L*ord, support us all the daylong of this troublous *life*, until the shadow lengthens, and the evening comes, and the busy world is hushed, and the fever of *life* is over, and our work is done. Then, of thy great mercy, grant us safe lodging and a holy rest, and peace at last; through Jesus Christ, our Lord. Amen.     *(Cardinal Newman)*

17. *Y*ou cannot control the length of your *life*, but you can control its width and depth. You cannot control the weather, but you can control the moral atmosphere that surrounds you. You can't control the other fellow's annoying faults, but you can see to it that you do not develop and harbour provoking propensities. You can't control hard times or rainy days, but you can bank money now to boost you through. Why worry about things you can't control? Get busy controlling the things that depend on you.     *(***)*

18. *P*eople love to complain about their problems, but are usually more stimulated than destroyed by them. *If* a man has no trouble to overcome, no dangers to surmount, no barriers to break through, how can he prove he's a hero? It is also better to have a choice of problems to worry about, as one problem can become too boring.     *(Hal Boyle)*

19. *We* are human. We are not perfect. We are alive. We try things. We make mistakes. We stumble. We

fall. We get hurt. We rise again. We keep learning. We keep growing.

And...

We are thankful for this priceless opportunity called **life.** *(***)*

20. ***Life*** is full of ups and downs. The trick is to enjoy the ups and have courage during the downs. *(***)*

21. ***Life's*** challenges are not supposed to paralyze you; they're supposed to help you discover who you are. *(**Bernice Johnson Reagan**)*

22. ***In*** this ***life*** we only get those things for which we hunt, for which we strive, and for which we are willing to sacrifice. *(**George Adams**)*

23. ***The*** amount of satisfaction you get from ***life*** depends largely on your own ingenuity, self - sufficiency, and resourcefulness. People who, wait around for life to supply their satisfaction usually find boredom instead. *(**William Menninger**)*

24. ***The*** people who usually get the most out of ***life*** are those who are prepared to roll with the punches... those who recognize the fact that they can't afford to become static and stagnant. The ability to adapt to new conditions is particularly important today. We have never lived in times when change has been swifter in almost every area of our lives. *(**Leon Kulikowski**)*

25. *A*n arrow can only be shut by pulling it backwards, so when **life** is pulling you back with difficulties, it means that it's going to launch you into something great. So, stay focused and keep aiming, and be happy, always! *(Xandria)*

26. *I* love the man that can smile in trouble, can gather strength from distress, and grow brave by reflection. It's the business of little minds to shrink, but he whose heart is firm, and whose conscience approves his conduct, will pursue his principles unto death. (***Thomas Paine***)

27. *T*he difficulties and struggles of today are but the best price we must pay for the accomplishments and victory of tomorrow. *(**William Boetcker**)*

28. *Y*ou will never stub your toe standing still. The faster you go, the more chance there is of stubbing your toe, but the more chance you have of getting somewhere. (***Charles F. Kettering***)

29. *A* ship is not made for a calm harbor and neither are we. (***Albert J. Nimeth***)

30. *I*nto each *life* some rain must fall. Some days must be dark and dreary (***Henry W. Longfellow***)

31. *T*he art of living lies less in eliminating our troubles than in growing with them.
(***Bernard M. Baruch***)

32. *T*he art of living is more like wrestling than dancing. (***Marcus Aurelius***)

33. *N*either as looser, nor as a sinner, in the battlefield of **life**, you emerge as a winner with your inclination, dedication and perspiration. Have a firm mind with a goal and reach your destination. Your path will be blocked by heavy perils and storm, surpass them with a will to succeed, impulsive and strong. Unjust situations will compel you to be rude, ignore them all bidding with a salute. If one hurts your conscience and degrades your pride, best you forgive and the least you fight. If the days are gloomy and the future becomes dark, be fearless as a tiger and cheerful as a lark. Then you won't be a looser, nor a sinner. But in the battlefield of **life**, you'll emerge as a winner. With your inclination, dedication and perspiration, and with a firm mind and goal, you would reach your destiny. **(Charles Menezes)**

34. *Y*ou desire to know the art of living, my friend? It is contained in one phrase: make use of suffering.
**(Henri-Frédéric Amiel)**

35. *W*ithout struggle, there is no progress. **(***)**

36. *E*very struggle in your **life** *has shaped you into the person you are today. Be thankful for the hard times; they have made you stronger.* **(***)**

37. *L*earn to roll with the storms of **life** and I'll see you at the top! **(Zig Ziglar)**

# CHAPTER TWO
## LIFE IS *"A JOURNEY"*

**L**ife is a journey, not a home; a road, not a city of habitation; and the enjoyments and blessings we have are but little inns on the roadside of *life*, where we may be refreshed for a moment that we may with new strength press on to the end, to the rest that remaineth for the people of God. It is not for man to trifle; *life* is brief, and sin is here. We have no time to sport away the hours; all must be earnest in a world like ours.

*(Bonar)*

2. **N**o matter how much you are hurt, always remember that "it is insignificant" because your journey together on the train of **life** is so short, irreversible, and its duration hidden from you. You need to have a good relationship with all the passengers on board in order to spice the journey.

*(***)*

3. **O**ur destination is home with our Father in heaven. It is so easy on this journey to lose sight of our destination and to focus on the detours of this **life** instead. This **life** is only the trip to get home.

*(Bob Snyder)*

4. **T**his journey through **life** can be a pleasant and rewarding experience if we have the right attitude. A good attitude is like cork – it can hold you up. A poor attitude is like lead – it can sink you.

*(L. Kenneth Wright)*

5. **E**vils in the journey of **life** are like the hills that alarm travelers on the road. Both appear great at a distance, but when we approach them, we find they are far less insurmountable than we had conceived. *(Charles Caleb Colton)*

6. **Life** is a one-way street. No matter how many detours you take, none of them leads back.

*(Isabel Moore)*

7. **L**ive your **life** each day as you would climb a mountain. An occasional glance towards the summit keeps the goal in mind, but many beautiful scenes are to be observed from each new vintage

point. Climb slowly, steadily, enjoy each passing moment; and the view from the summit will serve as a fitting climax for the journey.

**(*Harold V. Melchert*)**

8.  *Life* is currently described in one of four ways: a journey, a battle, a pilgrimage, or a race. Select your own metaphors, but the necessity of finishing is all the same. For if *life* is a journey, it must be completed. If *life* is a battle, it must be finished. If *life* is a pilgrimage, it must be concluded. And if **life** is a race it must be won.    (***The War Cry***)

9.  *Life* **is a race**. Don't whimper if the track is rough and the  goal is distant. One day you shall reach it. *Life* **is a voyage**. Don't complain if the storms batter the hull or the winds tatter to shreds the sails. One day you shall come to your heaven.
    *Life* **is growth**. Don't find fault if the seed lies smothered and submerged in the dark earth before it blooms and blossoms. One day you shall have your harvest.
    *Life* **is a pilgrimage**. Don't falter on the road through self-pity because stones cut your feet and leave your blood on the trail. One day you will come to Immanuel's land. The God who, through the boundless sky guides the flight of the sparrow, who builds the blind bird's nest, will see to it that in His good time you shall arrive.

**(*Joseph R. Sizoo*)**

10. *It* isn't necessary to fly over the South Pole, climb the Matterhorn, or swim the English Channel, to find adventure. *Life* itself is an adventure ....

Doing things that lift or steer humanity to higher levels is not only an adventure, but also a service to mankind and to God. **(Charlie "T" Jones)**

11. *It* is the way of the world, that when a human being is born, all rejoice; but when he dies, all sorrow. It should be the other way around. No one can tell what troubles await the developing child on its journey through *life*. But when a man has lived well and dies in peace, all should rejoice, for he has completed his journey successfully and he is departing from this world with the undying crown of a good name. **(*Midrash*)**

12. **A**t whatever crossroads you may now find yourself in *life*, it may be well to pause and ask yourself where you are on *life*'s journey; what you feel you have accomplished this far, or failed to accomplish; and what you think you have a right to expect, as a result of where you are, to bring into your future. **(*Harold Sherman*)**

13. **W**hat a large volume of adventure may be grasped within this little span of *life*, by him who interests his heart in everything, and who, having eyes to see what time and chance are perpetually holding out to him as he journeyed on his way, misses nothing he can fairly lay his hands on! **(*Laurence Sterne*)**

14. *Life* is a short walk. There is so little time and so much living to achieve. **(*John Oliver Killens*)**

15. *Life* is short and we have never too much time for gladdening the hearts of those who are traveling

the dark journey with us. Oh, be swift to love, make haste to be kind.   **(Henri-Frederic Amiel)**

16.  *T*o darken our journey together with quarrels, futile arguments, unforgiveness, ungratefulness and bad attitudes is unnecessary and a waste of time and energy                                          *(***)*

17. *A*ny road you travel in *life* is made infinitely better if you remember to pack a smile in your luggage and take it out frequently on your trip.

**(Anthony Vespugio)**

18. *Life* is one long process of getting tired.

**(Butler Samuel)**

19. *Life* is a dream for the wise, a game for the fool, a comedy for the rich, and a tragedy for the poor.
**(Sholom Aleichem)**

20. *Life* is like riding a bicycle. To keep your balance, you must keep moving.   **(Albert Einstein)**

21. *T*here is no beginning or end to your dreams or plans. *Life* is a journey from moment to moment. Live each moment to the fullest.

**(Garth Catterall-Heart)**

*22 Aitchison* summarizes this chapter with a soul-searching and an inspirational message:

*Life is like a journey on a train with its stations, with changes of routes and with accidents!*

*At birth we board the train and meet our parents, and we believe they will always travel on our side. However, at some station our parents will step down from the train, leaving us on this journey alone.*

*As time goes by, other people will board the train; and they will be significant i.e. our siblings, friends, children, and even the love of our **life**. Many will step down and leave a permanent vacuum. Others will go so unnoticed that we don't realize that they vacated their seats.*

*This train ride will be full of joy, sorrow, fantasy, expectations, hellos, goodbyes, and farewells.*

*Success consists of having a good relationship with all the passengers ... requiring that we give the best of ourselves. The mystery to everyone is: We do not know at which station we ourselves will step down.*

*So, we must live in the best way -*

*Love, forgive, and offer the best of who we are. It is important to do this because when the time comes for us to step down and leave our seat empty, we should leave behind beautiful memories for those who will continue to travel on the train of **life** without us.*

*I wish you a joyful journey for the coming years on your train of **life**. Reap success, give lots of love and be happy. More importantly, be thankful for the journey! Lastly, I thank you for being one of the passengers on my train.* **(Steven Aitchison)**

# CHAPTER THREE
## LIFE IS *"TAKING RISKS"*

**L***ife* without risks is not worth living.

**(*Charles A. Lindbergh*)**

*2.* **T**ake a chance!  All *life* is a chance. The man who goes farthest is generally the one who is willing to do and dare. **(*Dale Carnegie*)**

3. **A**ny *life* truly lived is a risky business, and if one puts up too many fences against risks, one ends up shutting out *life* itself. **(*Kenneth S. Davis*)**

4. **Y**ou cannot grow, in whatever direction, without taking risks, and if you have stopped growing, you

might as well be dead. You cannot know people without loving them, which brings its attendant risks of loss and pain. You cannot climb Mount Everest without risking your neck, and nothing can be achieved without risking time, effort, and reputation. **(*Eva Figes*)**

5. ***Life*** is not measured by the breaths you take, but by its breathtaking moments. **(*Michael Vance*)**

6 ***W*e** live by faith or we do not live at all. Either we venture—or we vegetate. If we venture, we do so by faith simply because we cannot know the end of anything at its beginning. We risk marriage on faith or we stay single. We prepare a profession by faith or we give up before we start. By faith we move mountains of opposition or we are stopped by molehills. **(*Harold Blake Walker*)**

7. ***T*he** effective person is seen as being able to commit himself to projects, investing time and energy and being willing to take appropriate economic, psychological and physical risks. He is seen as being able to think in different and original, that is, creative ways. Finally, he is able to control impulses and produce appropriate responses to frustration, hostility and ambiguity.
**(*Donald H. Blocher*)**

8. ***E*very** human being, for vitality, maturity, growth, and fulfillment, needs constant stress, constant risk, in order to reach his fullness as a creature. When you play it safe, as so many are trying to do — get a job and bury yourself in the soft,

amorphous womb of industry or some giant corporation, quite often you begin to lose the qualities that make a human being great or successful. You tend to relax; you tend to stop growing. *(Earl Nightingale)*

9. *D*on't be afraid to take a big step if one is indicated. You can't cross a chasm in two small jumps. *(David Lloyd George)*

10. *F*ar better to dare mighty things, to win glorious triumphs, even though checkered by failure, than to take rank with those poor spirits who neither enjoy much nor suffer much, because they live in the grey twilight that knows not victory or defeat. *(Theodore Roosevelt)*

11. *A life* spent making mistakes is not only more honourable but more useful than a *life* spent doing nothing. *(George Bernard Shaw)*

12. *T*he mistake riddled *life* is much richer, more interesting, and more stimulating than the *life* that has never risked or taken a stand on anything *(David McNally)*

13. *T*he world needs people... who do not have a price at which they can be bought; who do not borrow from integrity to pay for expediency; whose handshake is an ironclad contract; who are not afraid of risk; who have opinions instead of prejudices; who are as honest in large matters as in small ones; whose ambitions are big enough to include others; who know how to win with grace

and lose with dignity; who still have friends they made twenty years ago; who are occasionally wrong and always willing to admit it. **(***)**

14. *If* the creator had a purpose in equipping us with a neck, he surely meant us to stick it out.

**(Arthur Koestler)**

15. *T*here is risk in everything. **(Robert Schuller)**

16. *T*here is risk in not taking risks. **(Benson Idahosa)**

17. *T*ake risks. You can't fall off the bottom.

**(Barbara Proctor)**

18. *T*ake calculated risks. That is quite different from being rash. **(George S. Patton)**

19. *Y*ou don't concentrate on risk. You concentrate on results. No risk is too great to prevent the necessary job from getting done **(Chuck Yeager)**

20. *If* your *life* is ever going to get better, you'll have to take risks. There is simply no way you can grow without taking chances. **(David Viscot)**

21. *If* you don't risk anything, you risk even more.

**(Erica Jong)**

22. *P*eople who take risks are the people you'll lose against. **(John Scully)**

23. *Y*ou never know what you can do till you try.

**(McLaren, D.D.)**

24. *It*'s this simple: if I never try anything, I never learn anything. If I never take risks I stay where I am. **(Hugh Prather)**

25. *By* embracing risk, you will accomplish more than you ever thought you could. In the process, you will transform your *life* into an exciting adventure that will constantly challenge, reward, and rejuvenate you. **(Robert J. Krieger)**

26. *T*hings may come to those who wait, but only the things left by those who hustle. **(Abraham Lincoln)**

27. *O*ver the years, I have developed a picture of what a human being living humanely is like. She is a person who understands, values and develops her body, finding it beautiful and useful; a person who is real and is willing to take risks, to be creative, to manifest competence, to change when the situation calls for it, and to find ways to accommodate to what is new and different, keeping that part of the old that is still useful and discarding what is not. **(Virginia Satir)**

28. *Life* is not a spectacle or a feast; it is a predicament. **(George Santayana)**

29. *E*verything in *life* is luck. **(Donald Trump)**

30. *All* *life* is an experiment. The more experiments you make the better. **(Ralph Waldo Emerson)**

31. *Life* is "trying things to see if they work." **(Ray Bradbury)**

32. *D*are! And dare again! And go on daring.
**(George Danton)**

33. *N*othing will come of nothing. Dare mighty things.
**(Shakespeare)**

34. *I*t is not because things are difficult that we do not dare; it is because we do not dare that things are difficult.
**(Seneca)**

35. *O*nly those who dare to fail miserably can achieve greatly.
**(Robert Kennedy)**

36 *A*ttack *life*, it's going to kill you anyway.
**(Steven Coallier)**

37 *O*ne must work and dare if one really wants to live.
**(Vincent van Gogh)**

38. *I*f thou art a man, admire those who attempt great things even though they fail.
**(Seneca)**

39. *T*wenty years from now you will be more disappointed by the things you didn't do than by the ones you did do. So, throw off the bowlines. Sail away from the safe harbor. Catch the trade winds in your soils. Explore! Dream! Discover!
**(Mark Twain)**

40. *I*njustice can be eliminated, but human conflicts and natural limitations cannot be removed. The conflicts of social *life* and the limitations of nature cannot be controlled or transcended. They can, however, be endured and survived. It is possible

for there to be a dance with *life*, a creative response to its intrinsic limits and challenges.

**(Sharon Welch)**

41. *S*ecurity is mostly a superstition. It does not exist in nature, nor do the children of men as a whole experience it. Avoiding danger is no safer in the long run than outright exposure. **Life** is either a daring adventure or nothing.  **(Helen Keller)**

42. *M*any things are sweetened by risk.

**(Harry Millner)**

43. *S*erious harm, I am afraid, has been wrought to our generation by fostering the idea that they would live secure in a permanent order of things. They have expected stability and find non within themselves or in their universe. Before it is too late, they must learn and teach others that only by brave acceptance of change and all-time crisis ethics can they rise to the height of superlative responsibility.  **(Helen Keller)**

44. *T*he most important thing in *life* is the choice of a calling: it is left to chance.  **(Blaise Pascal)**

45. *I* think games are significant in people's lives because in a game everything is clearly defined. You've got the rules and a given period of time in which to play; you've got boundaries and a beginning and an end. And whether you win, lose, or draw, at least something is sure. But *life* isn't like that at all. So, I think people invent and play games in order to kid themselves, at least for a

time into thinking that **life** is a game.

**(James Jones)**

46. **T**wo roads diverged in a wood and I took the one less travelled by, and that has made all the difference. **(Robert Frost)**

47. **Life** is the art of drawing sufficient conclusions from insufficient premises. **(Butler Samuel)**

# CHAPTER FOUR
## LIFE IS *"SEIZING OPPORTUNITIES"*

*T*he greatest achievement of the human spirit is to live up to one's opportunities and make the most of one's resources.
**(Marquis De Vauvenargues)**

2. **G**od's best gift to us is not things, but opportunities. **(Alice W. Rollins)**

3. **G**reat opportunities come to all, but many do not know that they have met them. The only

preparation to take advantage of them is... to watch what each day brings.     **(Albert Dunning)**

4.  *E*very day comes bearing its own gifts. Untie the ribbons.                            **(Ruth Schabacker)**

5.  **Life** is not a collection bureau for power and wealth, but an opportunity for service.

    **(John W. Raley)**

6.  *T*he secret of success in **life** is for a man to be ready for his opportunity when it comes.

    **(Benjamen Disraeli)**

7.  *S*mall opportunities are usually the beginning of great enterprises.          **(Demosthenes)**

8.  *T*o improve the golden moment of opportunity, and catch the good that is within our reach, is the great art of **life**.          **(Samuel Johnson)**

9.  *T*he lesson which **life** repeats and constantly reinforces is 'look underfoot'. You are always nearer the divine and the true source of your power than you think. The lure of the distant and the difficult is deceptive. The greatest opportunity is where you are. Do not despise your own place and hour. Every place is under the stars, every place is the centre of the world.

    **(John Burroughs)**

10. *F*ortune knocks at every man's door once in a **life**, but in a good many cases the man is in a

neighbouring saloon and does not hear her.

**(Mark Twain)**

11. *O*pportunities are swarming around us all the time, thicker than gnats at sundown. We walk through a cloud of them. **(Henry Van Dyke)**

12. *A*n optimist sees an opportunity in every calamity ; a pessimist sees a calamity in every opportunity. **(Herbert V. Prochnow)**

13. *G*reat opportunities often disguise themselves in small tasks. **(Rick Warren)**

14. *I*n the middle of difficulty lies opportunity. **(Albert Einstein)**

15. *O*pportunity is missed by most because it is dressed in overalls and looks like work. **(Thomas Alva Edison)**

16. *I* make the most of all that comes and the least of all that goes. **(Sara Teasdale)**

17. *O*pportunities multiply as they are seized; they die when neglected. **(***)**

18. *O*ur real blessings often appear to us in the shapes of pains, losses and disappointments; but let us have patience, and we soon shall see them in their proper figures. **(Joseph Addison)**

19. *E*very time one door closes, another opens. God's delays are not God's denials. What looks like the end of the road will turn out to be a bend. **(***)**

20. *W*hen one door closes, another opens; but we often look so long and so regretfully upon the closed door that we do not see the one that has been opened for us. **(Alexander Graham Bell)**

21. *M*any do with opportunities as children do at seashore; they fill their little hands with sand, and then let the grains fall through, one by one, till all are gone. **(Zig Ziglar)**

22. *D*ifficulties mastered are opportunities won. **(Winston Churchill)**

23. *W*hat is the difference between an obstacle and an opportunity and our attitude toward it? Every opportunity has a difficulty, and every difficulty has an opportunity. **(J. Sidlow Baxter)**

24. *A*s bees extract honey from thyme, the strongest and driest of herbs, so sensible men often get advantage and profit from the most awkward circumstances. **(Plutarch)**

25. *M*ake the best use of thy prosperity, and then of thy reserves when they happen. For good and evil fortune come and go, revolving like a wheel insures rotation. **(Mahabharata)**

26. *O*pportunities do arrive, for everyone. Some **tips** for using them: Don't wait for the big opportunity. Small opportunities may expand. Keep in touch with what is going on, and be open-minded to new notions and ideas. Locate a real need. Check out the difficulties. Collect information. Then produce

the answer. Translate your plan into action as soon as possible. Do something beyond your regular and assigned duties. Opportunities are found through the little extras. Difficulties beset all beginnings. Persist. **(*Royal Bank of Canada Letter*)**

27. *W*hen you get into a tight place, and it seems you can't go on, hold on, for that's just the place and time the tide will turn. **(Harriet Beecher)**

28. *W*hen heaven is about to confer a great office on anyone, it first exercises his mind with suffering and his sinews and bones with toil; it exposes his body to hunger, and subjects him to extreme poverty, and it confounds his undertaking. In all these ways it stimulates his mind, hardens his nature and supplies his incompetency.

**(William McDougall)**

29. *F*or every man the world is as it was at the first day, and as full of untold novelties for him who has the eyes to see them. **(Thomas H. Huxley)**

30. *M*ediocre men wait for opportunities to come to them. Strong, able, alert men go after opportunity.

**(B.C. Forbes)**

# CHAPTER FIVE
## LIFE IS
## *"COURAGEOUSNESS"*

**C**ourage is the art of being the only one who knows you're scared to death. *(Earl Wilson)*

1.  **C**ourage is doing what you are afraid to do. There is no courage unless you are scared.
    **(Eddie Rickenacker)**

3.  **C**ourage is the firmness of Spirit that faces extreme danger or difficulty without flinching or retreating.
    **(Webster's Dictionary)**

4.  **O**ften the test of courage is not to die but to live.
    (**Alfieri – Orestes**)

5.  **I**f one advances confidently in the direction of his dreams, and endeavours to live the **life** that he has imagined, he will meet with a success unexpected in common hours.    (**Henry David Thoreau**)

6.  **I**t is a lovely thing to live with courage and die, leaving an everlasting flame.  (**Alexander the Great**)

7.  **W**hat would **life** be if we had no courage to attempt anything?    (**Vincent van Gogh**)

8.  **I**t isn't **life** that matters, but the courage you bring to it.    (**Hugh Walpole**)

9.  **P**eople grow through experience if they meet **life** honestly   and courageously. This is how character is built.    (**Eleanor Roosevelt**)

10. **W**hether you are man or woman, you will never do anything in this world without courage. It is the greatest quality of the mind next to honour.
    (**James Lane Allen**)

11. **W**hatever course you decide upon, there is always someone to tell you that you are wrong. There are always difficulties arising which tempt you to believe that your critics are right. To map out a course of action and follow it to an end requires ... courage.    (**Ralph Waldo Emerson**)

12. *C*ourage is the first of human qualities because it is the quality that guarantees all others.
**(Winston Churchill)**

13. *W*ithout courage, wisdom bears no fruit.
**(Balthazar Gracian)**

14. *H*owever mean your **life** is, meet it and live it; do not shun it and call it hard names. It is not as bad as you are. It looks poorest when you are richest. The fault finder will find faults even in paradise. Love your **life.**           **(Henry David Thoreau)**

15. *I*t takes courage to live–courage and strength and hope and humour. And courage and        strength and hope and humour have to be bought and paid for with pain and work and prayers and tears.
**(Jerome P. Fleishman)**

16. *K*eep your fears to yourself but share your courage with others.           **(Robert Louis Stevenson)**

17. *C*ourage is resistance to fear, mastery of fear, not absence of fear.           **(Mark Twain)**

18. *D*on't waste **life** in doubts and fear; spend yourself on the work before you, well assured       that the right performance of this hour's duties will be the best preparation for the hours and ages that will follow it.           **(Ralph Waldo Emerson)**

19 *T*here are two significant characteristics of a great **life**. The first is the capacity to make a good

beginning and the second is courage to push on to a good ending. *(***)*

20. *T*he only reason why you are not what you should be is that you don't dare to be. Once you dare, once you stop drifting with the crowd and face *life* courageously, *life* takes on a new significance. New forces take shape within you. You know you are a leader in one way or another; you know you are important to God and your fellowmen.

*(Charles E. Jones)*

21. *D*on't lose heart. Always preserve a healthy optimism. History is the teacher of *life*, and our past experiences school us for the future. A battle lost; we have time as long as we live to succeed in another. "All things work together for good", when there is good will. *(James Alberione)*

22. *D*on't be afraid to fail. Don't waste energy trying to cover up failure. Learn from your failures and go on to the next challenge. It's OK. If you're not failing, you're not growing. *(H. Stanley Judd)*

23. *B*e not afraid of *life*. Believe that *life* is worth living, and your belief will help create the fact.

*(***)*

24. *D*on't get discouraged; it is often the last key in the bunch that opens the lock. *(***)*

25. *S*uccess is never final and failure never fatal. It's courage that counts. *(***)*

26. *I*f you do not do the things you fear, then the fear controls your   *life.*                  *(Glenn Ford)*

27  *W*e must constantly build dykes of courage to hold back the flood of fear.        *(Martin Luther King, Jr.)*

28. *P*ut a grain of boldness in everything you do.
*(Balthazar Gracian)*

29. *O*ne of the saddest things in *life* is to see a man begin some worthy venture revealing great promise and then to watch him flounder into failure for lack of courage to push on through frustration and disappointment.   A *life* of triumph hinges on a firm faith for rugged times.  *(Harold Blake Walker)*

30. *W*hen things go wrong, as they sometimes will; when the road you are trudging seems all uphill; when the funds are low and the debts are high, and you want to smile, but you have to sigh;    when care is pressing you down a bit; rest if you must, but don't you quit. *Life* is queer with its twists and turns.                                              *(***)*

31. *I*s *life* so dear or peace so sweet as to be purchased at the price of chains and slavery? Forbid it, Almighty God! I know not what cause others may take; but as for me, give me liberty, or give me death.                                          *(Patrick Henry)*

32. *N*ever be bullied into silence. Never allow yourself to be made a victim. Accept no one's definition of your *life*; define yourself.        *(Harvey Fierstein)*

33. *I* am the good shepherd. A good shepherd lays down his *life* to save his sheep. If a hired man who is not a shepherd and has no sheep of his own sees the wolf coming, he abandons the sheep and runs away. **(Jesus –John 10:11-12)**

34. *If* my doctor told me I had only six minutes to live, I wouldn't  brood, and I'd type a little faster. **(Isaac Asimov)**

35. *It* is better to die on your feet than to live on  your knees! **(Emiliano Zapata)**

36. *It* is better to be a lion for a day than to be a sheep all your *life*. **(***)**

37. **W**hen faced with two dangers, one behind you and one in front     of you, it is always better to go forward. **(Zulu Saying)**

38. **T**he winds and waves are always on the side of the ablest navigators. **(***)**

39. **W**hatever you can do or dream, you can begin it. Boldness has genius, power and magic in it. Begin now! **(Goethe)**

# CHAPTER SIX
## LIFE IS
## *"DETERMINATION"*

*T*he difference between the impossible and the possible lies in a person's determination.
*(Tommy Lasorda)*

2. **N**ever say never. Never is a long, undependable thing, and **life** is full of rich possibilities to have restrictions placed upon it.　　*(Gloria Swanson)*

3. **D**etermination is the great quality that enables you to overcome all setbacks, disappointments, temporary failures, and every obstacle that throws in your path.　　*(Brian Tracey)*

4.  *If* a man hasn't discovered something he will die for, he isn't fit to live.     *(Martin Luther King Jr.)*

5.  *The* winners in *life* are people who, above all else, have determination.     *(Robert Seymour)*

6.  *A* determined person is one who, when he gets to the end of the rope, he ties a knot and hangs on.
     *(Joe L. Griffith)*

7.  *There* is no short cut to achievement. *Life* requires thorough preparation - veneer isn't worth anything.     *(George Washington Carver)*

8.  *We* must remember that one determined person can make a significant difference, and that a small group of determined people can change the course of history.     *(Sonia Johnson)*

9.  *Most* of the important things in the world have been accomplished by people who have kept on trying when there seemed to be no hope at all.
     *(Dale Carnegie)*

10. *Nothing* in this world can take the place of persistence. Talent will not; nothing is more common than unsuccessful men with talent. Genius will not; unrewarded genius is almost a proverb. Education will not; the world is full of educated derelicts. Persistence and determination alone are omnipotent.     *(Calvin Coolidge)*

11. *S*uccess in *life* is a matter not so much of talent or opportunity, as of concentration and perseverance.
*(C.W. Wendte)*

12. *S*tick to the fight when you're hardest hit. It's when things seem worst that you must not quit.
*(***)*

13. *P*erseverance is the ingredient of *life* that sometimes makes up for lack of genius.
*(W. Ballentine Henley)*

14. *S*ome men succeed because they are destined to, but most men because they are determined to.
*(***)*

15. *I* care not that you failed. I care whether you are content to remain there.  *(Abraham Lincoln)*

16. *N*othing is more expensive than a start.
*(Nietzsche)*

17. *I*t is never too late to be what you might have been.  *(George Eliot)*

18. *O*ne may walk over the highest mountain one step at a time.  *(John Wanamaker)*

19. *K*eep your light shining; tiny lights guide even great ships into harbor.  *(***)*

20. *B*e like a duck - keep calm and unruffled on the surface, but paddle like crazy underneath.  *(***)*

21. *R*uthlessly compete with your own best self.
*(Apollo 13 Engineers)*

22. *T*o get through the hardest journey, we need take only one step at a time, but we must keep on stepping. **(***)**

23. **K**eep trying. It's only from the valley that the mountain seems high. **(***)**

24. *I*t's only when we truly know and understand that we have a limited time on earth – and that we have no way of knowing when our time is up – that we will begin to live each day to the fullest, as if it was the only one, we had. **(Elisabeth Kubler-Ross)**

25. *M*y formula for living is quite simple. I get up in the morning and I go to bed at night. In between, I occupy myself as best I can. **(Cary Grant)**

26. *I* don't want to get to the end of my *life* and find that I lived just the length of it. I want to have lived the width of it as well. **(Diane Ackerman)**

27. *M*ake plans as if you were going to live forever; live as if it were the last day of your *life* on earth. **(***)**

28. *L*ive everyday as if it were your last. Do every job as if you were the boss. Drive as if all other vehicles were police cars. Treat everyone else as if he were you. **(Charles Menezes)**

29. *U*se your eyes as if tomorrow you will be stricken blind; hear, touch, smell, and taste as if tomorrow you would lose all these senses. Make the most of every sense. **(Helen Keller)**

30. *L*ive every act fully as if it were your last. *(Buddha)*

31. *A*nd thou wilt give thyself relief, if thou doest every act of thy *life* as if it were the last.

*(Marcus Aurelius)*

32. *W*ork like you don't need the money, love like your heart has never been broken, and dance like no one is watching. *(Aurora Greenway)*

33. *Y*ou've got to sing like you don't need the money. You've got to love like you'll never get hurt. You've got to dance like there's nobody watching. You've got to come from the heart, if you want it to work. *(Susanna Clark)*

34. *W*ork as though you would live forever, and live as though you would die today. *(Og Mandino)*

35. *L*ive as if you were to die tomorrow. Learn as if you were to live forever. *(Mahatma Gandhi)*

36. *W*hen faced with a mountain, I will not quit! I will keep on striving until I climb over, find a pass through, tunnel underneath —or simply stay and turn the mountain into a gold mine, with God's help! *(Robert Schuller, Sr.)*

37. *W*e shall not fail or falter; we shall not weaken or tire …. Give us the tools and we will finish the job. *(Winston Churchill)*

38. *T*he art of living successfully consists of being able to hold two opposite ideas in tension at the same time: First, to make long-term plans as if we were

going to live forever. And second, to conduct ourselves daily as if we were going to die tomorrow. **(Sydney J. Harris)**

39. **A**lways try to drive so your license will expire before you do. **(***)**

40. **T**he fellow who succeeds above his mates is the one who early in **life**, discerns his object and towards that object habitually directs his powers. **(Sir Edward Lytton)**

41. **Life** can be one dreary day after another or a Baghdad of fascinating things to keep learning. Get more out of every phase of your **life** – stay incurably curious. **(L. Perry Wilbur)**

42. **W**elcome change as a friend; try to visualize new possibilities and the blessings it is bound to bring you…. Never stop learning and never stop growing; that is the key to a rich and fascinating **life**. **(Alexander de Seversky)**

43. **T**he heights great men reached and kept were not attained by sudden flights, but they, while their companions slept, were toiling upward in the night. **(Henry W. Longfellow)**

44. **B**ite off more than you can chew, and then chew it. Plan more than you can do, then do it. Point your arrow at a star, take your aim, and there you are. Arrange more time than you can spare, then spare it. Take on more than you can bear, then

bear it. Plan your castle in the air, then build a ship to take you there. **(***)**

45. *T*housands of men have been failures in **life** because they did not go quite far enough. They did not learn a trade to the point of efficiency!

**(Marden O. S.)**

46. *I* want to be thoroughly used up when I die, for the harder I work, the more I live. **Life** is no brief candle for me. It is a sort of splendid torch which I have got hold of for the moment and I want to make it burn as brightly as possible before handing it on to future generations. **(George Bernard Shaw)**

47. *W*henever your **life** ends it is all there. The advantage of living is not measured by length, but by use; some men have lived long, and lived little; attend to it while you are in it. It lies in our will, not in the number of years, for you to have lived enough. **(Montaigne)**

48. *I*f you can't be a highway, then just be a trail. If you can't be the sun, then be a star. It isn't by size that you win or fail. Be the best of whatever you are! **(Douglas Malloch)**

49. *W*e will have a better **life** if we make the most of the best and the least of the worst. **(***)**

50. *Y*ou have got to do your own growing, no matter how tall your grandfather was. **(***)**

51. **A**ll things come to him who waits, but the man who goes for what he wants gets it all the quicker.

*(***)*

52. **D**estiny is not a matter of chance, it is a matter of choice; it is not a thing to be waited for, it is a thing to be achieved. **(William Jenings Bryan)**

53. **I**f you're walking down the right path and you're willing to keep walking, eventually you'll make progress. **(Barack Obama)**

54. **B**ig shots are only little shots that keep shooting. **(Christopher Morley)**

55. **G**ood luck is another name for tenacity of purpose. **(Ralph Waldo Emerson)**

56. **T**oday's mighty oak is just yesterday's nut that held its ground. *(***)*

57. **Life** is great to every man who lives to do the best he can. *(***)*

58. **I**t is a funny thing about *life*: if you refuse to accept anything but the best, you very often get it. **(Somerset Maugham)**

59. **N**o matter what your lot in *life* is, build something on it. *(***)*

60. **Life** is what is happening while you are too busy to notice. *(***)*

61. *A*lways look at *life* through the binoculars of possibility. Run until you break the tape!     *(***)*

62. *P*lay every play as if it were going to be the game-breaker.     *(***)*

63. *B*elieve that *life* is worth living and your belief will help create the fact.     *(William James)*

64. *H*old fast to dreams, for if dreams die, then *life* is like a broken-winged bird that cannot fly.
*(Langston Hughes)*

65. *P*lan purposefully; prepare prayerfully; proceed positively; pursue persistently.     *(W.A. Ward)*

66. *T*hose who paid the price reached their goal.
*(John C. Maxwell)*

67. *S*o, live your *life* that your autograph will be wanted, not your fingerprints.     *(***)*

# CHAPTER SEVEN
## LIFE IS *"STRIKING AT A BALANCE"*

**I**f a man is to live a full *life*, an appropriate amount of physical activity must be mixed with mental activity and spiritual activity. Without the existence of spiritual activity, man's *life* would be void. Without mental activity, man would be numb. Without physical activity, man would be vegetable. **(Linus Dowell)**

2. *E*ven as seasons bring sunshine and rain, **Life** must be balanced with gladness & pain. Even as trials seem heavy to bear, God sends His rainbow- a promise to care. Strength for the trials and help for the day, Rest for the journey and light for the way. Peace for the weary, and grace from above— God sends His promise of wonderful love!   *(***)*

3. *T*here are as many nights as days, and the one is just as long as the other in the year's course. Even a happy *life* cannot be without a measure of darkness and the word 'happy' would lose its meaning if it were not balanced by sadness.

   *(Carl Jung)*

4. *L*earning how to be strong, intelligent and balanced, how to resist fatigue and how to avoid making oneself detestable to others is no less essential than eating, sleeping, studying at school or working in the office, farm, or factory.

   *(Alexis Carrel)*

5. *T*he balanced person is self-contained. Neither is he subject to quick emotional reactions, nor does he jump to impulsive conclusions. The balanced one is resilient and flexible. Like the willow tree in the wind, he bends without breaking. He meets despair with hope, sorrow with equanimity.   *(***)*

6. *M*any people think that success in one area can compensate for failure in other areas. But can it really?... True effectiveness requires balance.   *(***)*

7.  **W**ork, love, and play are the great balance–wheels of man's being. **(Orison Swett Marden)**

8.  **I**f **life** does not give all that you want, rejoice that you are alive. Be sober, take a medium course to all things, so long as **life** lasts and then rest contented to leave behind a respected name. **(***)**

9.  **O**ne ought, every day at least, to hear a little song, read a good poem, see a fine picture, and, if it were possible, to speak a few reasonable words.
    **(Johann Wolfgang von Goethe)**

10. **H**ow shall I behave among the wise and the foolish, friends and strangers, the old and the young, and the innocent and the wicked?
    Be not too wise, nor too foolish;
    Be not too conceited, nor diffident;
    Be not too talkative, nor too feeble.
    If you be too wise, men will expect too much of you;
    If you be too conceited, you will be deceived;
    If you be too humble, you will be thought vexatious;
    If you be too talkative, you will not be heeded;
    If you be too silent, you will not be regarded;
    If you be too hard, you will be broken;
    If you be too feeble, you will be crushed.
    **(King Cormac)**

11. **I**t is the contrast between the dark and the light which gives **life** both its pathos and its glory.
    **(William Barclay)**

12. *L*ive within your means, financially, physically and mentally, and you stand the best chance there is of having both a happy *life* and plenty of years to enjoy it. **(*Dr. Kapphan*)**

13. *W*here there is charity and wisdom, there is neither fear nor ignorance. Where there is patience and humility, there is neither anger nor vexation. Where there is poverty and joy, there is neither greed nor avarice. Where there is peace and meditation, there is neither anxiety nor doubt.
**(*St. Francis of Assisi*)**

14. *B*itterness imprisons *life*; love releases it. Bitterness paralyses *life*; love empowers it. Bitterness sours *life*; love sweetens it. Bitterness sickens *life*; love heals it. Bitterness blinds *life*; love anoints its eyes. **(*Harry Emerson Fosdick*)**

15. *K*eep your eyes on the stars, and your feet on the ground. **(*Theodore Roosevelt*)**

16. *P*atience is bitter but its fruit is sweet. **(*Rousseau*)**

17. *M*an seeks fulfillment in the sweet things of *life* only to find sadness. **(*****)**

18. *U*nhappiness is man's inheritance; all of us are bound to be sad and even grief-stricken at times. The capacity to feel sad is perhaps just the other side of the capacity to feel happy. So, the most useful thing we can teach is that *life* is complex and difficult and the more roses you seek, the

likely you are to fall upon thorns.

**(*Elaine Cumming*)**

19. ***A*** little pain, a little pleasure, a little heaping up of treasure; then no more gazing upon the sun. All things must end that have begun.     **(*John Payne*)**

20. ***F*or everything there is a season:
    a time to be born and a time to die,
    a time to plant and a time to uproot,
    a time to break down and a time to build up,
    a time to mourn and a time to laugh,
    a time to seek and a time to lose,
    a time to keep and a time to cast away,
    a time to keep silence and a time to speak,
    a time to love and a time to hate,
    a time for war and a time for peace.     *(***)*

21. ***T*he happiest people are rarely the richest, or the most beautiful, or even the most talented. Happy people do not depend on excitement and fun supplied by externals. They enjoy the fundamental, often very simple, things of *life*. They waste no time thinking other pastures are greener; they do not yearn for yesterday or tomorrow. They savor the moment, glad to be alive, and enjoy their work, their families, and the good things around them. They are adaptable, they can bend with the wind, adjust to the changes in their times, enjoy the contests of *life*, and feel themselves in harmony with the world.     **(*Jane Canfield*)**

22.  **Y**ou cannot strengthen the weak by weakening the strong. You cannot help the wage-earner by pulling down the wage-payer. You cannot help the poor by destroying the rich. You cannot help men permanently by doing for them what they could and should do for themselves. (*Abraham Lincoln*)

23. **A**nd we should consider every day lost on which we have not danced at least once. And we should call every truth false which was not accompanied by at least one laugh.          (*Friedrich Nietzsche*)

24. **I**n the relentless busyness of modern *life*, we have lost the rhythm between action and rest.
(*Wayne Muller*)

25. **Y**ou have to pay the price. You will find that everything in *life* exacts a price, and you will have to decide whether the price is worth the prize.
(*Sam Nunn*)

# CHAPTER EIGHT
## LIFE IS *"TIME"*

**D**ost thou love *life?* Then do not squander time: for that is the stuff *life* is made of. **(Benjamin Franklin)**

2.  **Life** is all about timing… the unreachable becomes reachable, the unavailable becomes available, and the unattainable becomes the attainable. Have the patience! Wait it out! It's all about timing.

**(Stacey Charter)**

3.  *T*ime is the coin of your *life*. It is the only coin you have and only you can determine how it will be spent. Be careful lest you let other people spend it for you.                    **(Lady B. Johnson)**

4.  *H*alf our *life* is spent trying to find something to do with the time we have rushed through *life* trying to save.                    **(Will Rogers)**

5.  *Life* is a checkerboard, and the player apposite you is time. If you hesitate before moving or neglect to move promptly, your men will be wiped off the board by time. You are playing against a partner who will not tolerate indecision.    **(Napoleon Hill)**

6.  *T*ime changes everything, but you change everything by what you do with the time you have.                    **(Myles Munroe)**

7.  *B*ut what is this thing called time? It is *life*'s richest gift. It is intangible and evasive, yet ever with us, sometimes against us, sometimes with us. Sometimes we have it on our hands, other times we waste it. At times we have no time to lose, at others we have none to spare. We can be irregular in our time. Time never. We can be early or late, not so time. We can clock it but never stop it. It is an indestructible trinity: past, present, future. We may mistime our appointment but time never lets us down. We can share it with loved ones, endure it with enemies. All things fade into it: loves joys, pain and sorrow, gain and loss. It tests us and blesses us. "Our times are in His hands."   Oh!

Time Immemorial, I would that my moments and days are never wasted or ill spent. My times are in His hands who changes not. **(***)**

8. **Life** isn't a matter of milestones but of moments.
**(Rose Fitzgerald)**

9. **Life** is action and passion; therefore, it is required of a man that he should share the passion and action of his time at peril of being judged not to have lived. **(Oliver Wendell Holmes)**

10. **A** man who dares to waste one hour of time has not discovered the value of **life**. **(Charles Darwin)**

11. **The** most valuable gift one person can give another is time. **(Steve Weber)**

12. *The greatest gift you could ever give someone is your time. Your time for someone can help change their entire life, can wipe away the tears from their faces and can release them off their pains and tragedies.* **(***)**

13. **Time** is a companion that goes with us on a journey. It reminds us to cherish each moment, because it will never come again. What we leave behind is not as important as how we have lived.
**(Captain Jean-Luc Picard)**

14. **Time** does not become sacred to us until we have lived it, until it has passed over us and taken with it a part of ourselves. **(John Burroughs)**

15. *T*ime is a versatile performer. It flies, marches on, heals all wounds, runs out, and will tell.
**(Franklin P. Jones)**

16. *H*ow we spend our days is, of course, how we spend our lives. **(Annie Dillard)**

17. *B*e wise in the use of time. The question of *life* is not, "How much time have we?" The question is, "What shall we do with it?"
**(Anna Robertson Brown)**

18. *P*erfection is attained by degrees; it requires the hand of time. **(Voltaire)**

19. *T*o waste time is to waste your *life*, but to master your time is to master your *life*. **(***)**

20. *L*ike all things, time must be managed.
**(Aristotle)**

21. *L*ost time is never found. **(Benjamin Franklin)**

22. **Your** time is limited, so don't waste it living someone else's *life*. Don't be trapped by dogma - which is living with the results of other people's thinking. Don't let the noise of other's opinions drown out your own inner voice. And most importantly, have the courage to follow your heart and intuition. They somehow already know what you truly want to become. Everything else is secondary. **(Steve Jobs)**

23. *G*et into the habit of living according to plan. Allow yourself a sufficient margin of time in which

to do things. Leave nothing to chance. Hurry, worry and anxiety defeat your purpose. Eliminate from your *life*, as far as possible, all undue nervous strain, tension and excitements and you will accumulate great reserves of mental and physical vitality. **(Grenville Kleiser)**

24. *I* wish I could stand on a busy corner, hat in hand, and beg people to throw me all their wasted hours. **(Bernard Berenson)**

25. *T*ime slips through our hands like grains of sand, never to return again. Those who use time wisely are rewarded with rich, productive and satisfying lives. **(Robin Sharma)**

26. *S*o, the sands of time that slowly flow from out of my hourglass will all too soon have ebbed away. My *life* will then be past. So, I must make the most of time, and drift not with the tide, for killing time's not murder. It's more like suicide. **(***)**

27. *D*uring a very busy *life* I have often been asked, "How did you manage to do it all?" The answer is simple: Because I did everything promptly. **(Richard Tangye)**

28 *Life* is like an onion; you peel it off one layer at a time, and sometimes you weep. **(Carl Sandburg)**

29. *N*othing great is created suddenly, any more than a bunch of grapes or a fig. If you tell me that you desire a fig, I answer you that there must be time.

Let it first blossom, then bear fruits, then ripen.

*(Epictetus)*

30. *I* still find each day too short for all the thoughts I want to think, all the walks I want to take, all the books I want to read, and all the friends I want to see. *(John Burroughs)*

31. *T*here is no explanation quite so effective as silence. Explanations rarely explain. If you are right, your *life* will do its own explaining; if you are wrong, you can't explain. So, go calmly on your way and forget everything but the business of right living – and let time explain for you.

*(A. P. Gouthey)*

32. *W*e live in deeds not years; in thoughts, not breaths; in feelings, not in figures on the dial; we should count time by the heart-throbs. He most lives who thinks most, feels the noblest, and acts the best. *(Gamaliel Bailey)*

33. *Life* is short and we never have enough time for gladdening the hearts of those who travel the way with us. Oh, be swift to love! Make haste to be kind. *(Henri-Frédéric Amiel)*

34. *T*he value of *life* lies, not in the length of days, but in the use, we make of them. A man may live long, yet live very little. Satisfaction in *life* depends not on the number of your years, but on your will.

*(***)*

35. *T*o realize the VALUE OF ONE YEAR, ask a student who has failed the final exam.

    *T*o realize the VALUE OF ONE MONTH, ask a mother who has given birth to a premature baby.

    *T*o realize the VALUE OF ONE DAY, ask a blind man the beauty of the last of the millennium's last Solar Eclipse.

    *T*o realize the VALUE OF ONE HOUR, ask the lovers who are waiting to meet.

    *T*o realize the VALUE OF ONE MINUTE, ask a person who has missed the train, bus, or plane.

    *T*o realize the VALUE OF ONE MILLISECOND, ask the athlete who has won a Silver Medal in the Olympics.
    **(*Times of India Internet Humour*)**

36. **Life** can only be understood backwards; but it must be lived forwards. **(*Kierkegaard*)**

37. *T*ime is infinite movement without one moment of rest. **(*Tolstoy*)**

38. *T*ime is a river – flowing from the past to the future. **(***)**

39. **O**ur **life** is short, but to expand that span to vast eternity is virtue's work. **(*Shakespeare*)**

40. **W**hoever in middle age attempts to realize the hopes and wishes of his early youth, invariably deceives himself. Each ten years of a man's **life** has its own fortunes, its own hopes, and its own desires. **(*Goethe*)**

41. *Y*outh looks ahead, old age looks back, and middle age looks tired. *(***)*

42. *Y*outh is blunder; manhood is struggle; and old age is regret. *(Benjamin Disraeli)*

43. This time, like all times, is a very good one, if we but know what to do with it.
*(Ralph Waldo Emerson)*

44. *T*ime is a great teacher, but unfortunately, it kills all its pupils. *(Louis Hector Berlioz)*

# CHAPTER NINE
## LIFE IS *"THE PAST, PRESENT AND FUTURE"*

*I*t is never wise to live in the past. There are, indeed, some uses of our past which are helpful, and which bring blessing.... We should remember past failures and mistakes, that we may not repeat them. We should remember past mercies.... We should remember past comforts.... But while there are these true uses of memory, we should guard against living in the past. We should draw our *life*'s inspirations not from memory but from hope, from what is yet to come.

*(J. R. Miller)*

2. *S*implify your *life*. Don't waste the years struggling for things that are unimportant. Don't destroy

your peace of mind by looking back, worrying about the past. Live in the present, enjoy the present. Simplify! **(Henry David Thoreau)**

3. **Life** begins each morning. ... Each night of **life** is a wall between today and the past. Each morning is the open door to a new world – new vistas, new aims, and new tryings. **(Leigh Mitchell Hodges)**

4. **Listen to the Exhortation of the Dawn!**

Look to this Day! For it is **Life**, the very **Life** of **Life**.

In its brief course lies all the Verities and Realities of your Existence; the Bliss of Growth, the Glory of Action, and the Splendor of Beauty. Yesterday is but a Dream, and To-morrow is only a Vision. To-day well lived makes every Yesterday a Dream of Happiness, and every Tomorrow a Vision of Hope. Look well therefore to this Day! Such is the Salutation of the Dawn! **(Kalidasa)**

5. You can't bring back yesterday,
   You can't look into tomorrow.
   So, the only gift you have is today.
   That is why it's called the present. **(***)**

6. **Life** can be found only in the present moment. The past is gone, the future is not yet here, and if we do not go back to ourselves in the present moment, we cannot be in touch with **life**.
   **(Thich Nhat Hanh)**

7.  *Y*our past cannot be changed, but you can change your tomorrow by your actions today.

    **(David McNally)**

8.  *D*o not dwell in the past; do not dream of the future; concentrate the mind on the present moment.                              **(Buddha)**

9   *L*ove the moment. Flowers grow out of dark moments. Therefore, each moment is vital. It affects the whole.  **Life** is a succession of such moments and to live each, is to succeed.

    **(Corita Kent)**

10. **W**e are not living in eternity. We have only this moment, sparkling like a star in our hand – and melting like a snowflake. Let us use it before it is too late.                     **(Marie Beynon Ray)**

11. *N*ow is the watchword of the wise.

    **(Charles H. Spurgeon)**

12. **W**ipe out the past, trust the future, and live in a glorious now.                      **(Elizabeth Towne)**

13. **L**iving in the past is a dull and lonely business; looking back strains the neck muscles, causing you to bump into people not going your way.

    **(Edna Ferber)**

14. *I* regret nothing in my life.
    Even if my past was full of hurt,
    I still look back and smile, because it made me who I am today.                      **(***)**

15. **Be** *thankful for* everybody in your **life**, Good or Bad, Past or Present. They made you what you are today. **(***)**

16. **T**he past is a bucket of ashes, so live not in your yesterdays, nor just for tomorrow, but in the here and now. Keep moving and forget the post-mortems. **(Carl Sandburg)**

17. **D**o not judge the future by the past. In the past may be wisdom, but in the future is **life** and the miracles of the living which know no end. The past has experiences, but the future has surprises. The past produces memories, but the future produces expectation and hope…. The past is closed, but the future is open. **(Ben Nathan)**

18. **I**t is good to appreciate that **life** is now. Whatever it offers, little or much, **life** is now – this day–this hour. **(Charles Macomb Flandrau)**

19. **B**anish the future, live only for the hour and its allotted work. Think not the amount to be accomplished, the difficulties to be overcome, but set earnestly at the little task at your elbow, letting that be sufficient for the day; for surely our plain duty is "not to use what lies dimly at a distance, but to do what lies clearly at hand". **(Sir William Osler)**

20. **I** can feel guilty about the past, apprehensive about the future, but only in the present can I act. The ability to be in the present is a major component of mental wellness. **(Abraham Maslow)**

21  **O**ne of the illusions of **life** is that the present hour is not the critical, decisive hour. Write it on your heart that every day is the best day of the year.
**(Ralph Waldo Emerson)**

22  **I**t is wise to think about the past and learn from it. But it is unwise for us to be in the past …. It is also wise for us to think about the future and plan for it. But it is unwise for us to be in the future…. The present moment is the only reality we will ever experience.  **(Spencer Johnson)**

23.  **D**on't waste today regretting yesterday instead of making a memory for tomorrow.  **Laura Palmer)**

24  **Y**ou can't have a better tomorrow if you are thinking about yesterday all the time.
**(Charles F. Kettering)**

25.  **T**ime and **life** are made up of one today after another. Yesterday is a fallen leaf; tomorrow is still a dream; but today is here.  **(Esther Baldwin York)**

26.  **T**omorrow **life** is late; live today.  **(Martial)**

27.  **O**ne day, today, is worth two tomorrows.
**(Benjamin Franklin)**

28.  *T*oday is **life** - the only **life** you are sure of. Make the most of today.  Get interested in something. Shake yourself awake. Develop a hobby. Let the winds of enthusiasm sweep through you. Live today with gusto.  **(Dale Carnegie)**

29. **D**o not look back on happiness or dream of it in the future. You are only sure of today; do not let yourself be cheated out of it

**(Henry Ward Beecher)**

30. **I** believe in today. It is all that I possess. The past is of value only as it can make the **life** of today fuller and freer. There is no assurance of tomorrow. I must make good today!

**(Charles Stelzle)**

31. **T**oday is the tomorrow you worried about yesterday. **(***)**

32. **Life** is lived in the present. Yesterday has gone, tomorrow is yet to be. Today is the miracle. **(***)**

33. **T**oday gives us a chance to love, to work, to play, and to look up at the stars. **(Henry Van Dyke)**

34. **O**ur beliefs in a rich future **life** are of little importance unless we coin them into a rich present **life**. **(Thomas Dreier)**

35. **T**he future that we study and plan for begins today. **(Chester O. Fischer)**

36. **T**he flowers of all tomorrows are in the seeds of today. **(Chinise Proverb)**

37. **T**he future does not belong to those who are content with today. Rather, it belongs to those who can blend vision, reason and courage in a personal commitment. **(Robert Kennedy)**

38. *L*ive one day at a time. You can plan tomorrow and hope for the future, but don't live in it. Live this day well and tomorrow's strength will come tomorrow. **(Charles W. Shedds)**

39. *F*or yesterday is but a dream, and tomorrow is only a vision. But today, well-lived, makes yesterday a dream of happiness and every tomorrow a vision of hope. Look well, therefore, to this day. **(Sanskrit Proverb)**

40. *T*he best preparation for tomorrow is to do today's work superbly well. **(William Osler)**

41. *I* like the dreams of the future better than the history of the past. **(Thomas Jefferson)**

42. *S*top looking at where you have been and start looking at where you can be. **(Mike Murdock)**

43. *W*e should concentrate on doing with all our might and mind the thing that lies at hand, doing our best hour by hour, day by day, fretting as little as possible about what the future may hold or indulging too much in vain regrets over the past. **(B.C. Forbes)**

44. *S*uccess is reached by being active, awake, ahead of the crowd; by aiming high, pushing ahead honestly, diligently, patiently; by climbing, digging, saving; by forgetting the past, using the present, trusting in the future; by honouring God, having a purpose, fainting not, determining to win, and striving to the end. **(Russell Conwell)**

45. **To** understand one's self, we must study man's past. To understand the past, one must examine the relationship between systems of communication, transportation, philosophy, political structure, religion, science, climate and terrain, and on and on. **Life** is interwoven, not compartmentalized. **(Harry Kershen)**

46. **Bo**dily exercise is profitable to little: but godliness is profitable to all things, having promise of the **life** that now is, and of that which is to come.
**(1 Tim. 4:8)**

47. **Life** is not a having and a getting, but a being and a becoming. **(M. Arnold)**

48. **The** acts of this **life** are the destiny of the next.
**(Proverb)**

49. **There** is a past that is gone forever, but there is a future that is still our own. **(***)**

50. **We** sleep, but the loom of **life** never stops; and the pattern that was weaving when the sun went down is weaving when it comes up tomorrow.
**(Henry Ward Beecher)**

51. **To**morrow is the day when idlers work, and fools reform, and mortal men lay hold of heaven.
**(***)**

52 **The** future belongs to those who believe in the beauty of their dreams. **(Bart Forbes)**

53. **Wi**se men of today face the future unafraid.
**(Ernest C. Wilson)**

54. *My* interest is in the future because I am going to spend the rest of my *life* there.

**(Charles F. Kettering)**

55. *N*obody gets to live *life* backward. Look ahead; that is where your future lies.     **(Ann Landers)**

56. *Y*our future contains more happiness than any past you can remember.     **(John Mason)**

57  *T*he future is not a gift – it is an achievement.

**(Harry Lauder)**

58. *It* is difficult to live in the present, ridiculous to live in the future, and impossible to live in the past.

**(Jim Bishop)**

59. *F*rom Freud, we learned that the past exists now in the person. Now we must learn from growth theory and self-actualization theory that the future also now exists in the person in the form of ideals, hopes, goals, unrealized potentials, mission, fate, destiny, etc. One for whom no future exists is reduced to the concrete, to helplessness, to emptiness. For him, time must be endlessly filled. Striving, the usual organizer of most activity, when lost, leaves the person unorganized and uninterested.     **(Abraham H. Maslow)**

60. **Life** is a process. We are a process. The universe is a process.     **(Anne Wilson Schaef)**

# CHAPTER TEN
## LIFE IS *"BEYOND BIRTH & DEATH"*

**H**e that lives to live forever, never fears dying.

*(Penn)*

2. *N*o matter your social status or how powerful you feel you are, we are all equal. We came here by birth and will leave by death.          *(***)*

3. *I* think of death as a glad awakening from this troubled sleep, which we call *life*, as emancipation

75

from a world, which, beautiful though it be, is still a land of captivity. **(L. Abbott)**

4.  *T*hink not of death as the extinguishing of *life*, but rather the snuffing out of a candle because dawn has come. **(***)**

5.  *W*e must live under a constant apprehension of the shortness and uncertainty of *life*, and the near approach of death and eternity. **(Charles H. Spurgeon)**

6.  *T*his world is the land of the dying; the next is the land of the living. **(Tyron Edwards)**

7.  *S*ome people are so afraid to die that they never begin to live. **(Henry Van Dyke)**

8.  *I*n reality, death, which is sometimes so much feared, is for me, one of the most anticipated events, an event that will give meaning to my *life*. Death can be considered an end of *life* or as the threshold of eternity. In both these aspects, I find consolation... the final amen of any *life* and the first alleluia of eternity. **(Pedro Arrupe)**

9.  *P*eople living deeply have no fear of death. **(Anais Vin)**

10. *Life* and death are but one thing. You live and then you die. **(Alice Summer)**

11. *T*here is no cure for birth and death, save to enjoy the interval. **(George Santayana)**

12. *T*he truth is that we live and die. We have no control when we're born and when we leave this earth but we have absolute control over how we live each day in between. Live a quality *life* and do that by not waiting for the perfect future to arrive. Choose to be happy, always! **(Xandria)**

13. *W*e are born to accumulate fame and then to die and leave the world a better place than we met it.

    **(***)**

14. *H*e, who fears death while he lives, lives in death.

    **(***)**

15. *W*hile you do not know *life*, what can you know about death? **(Confucius)**

16. *T*hose who live as if they will never die, when they die, it is as if they never lived. **(***)**

17. *W*hen I go down in the grave I can say like many others: 'I have finished my day's work' – but I cannot say 'I have finished my *life.*' **(Victor Hugo)**

18. *W*hen a man is dead, they put money in his coffin, erect monuments to his memory, and celebrate the anniversary of his birthday in set speeches. Would they take notice of him if he were living? No!

    **(William Hazlitt)**

19. **D**eath is necessary and, it will come when it will come. **(William Shakespeare)**

20. *B*elief in immortality gives dignity to *life* and enables us to endure cheerfully those trials which come to us all. **(Samuel M. Lindsay)**

21. **D**eath is the golden key that opens the palace of eternity. *(John Milton)*

22. **B**irth, *life*, and death – each took place on the hidden side of a leaf. *(Toni Morrison)*

# CHAPTER ELEVEN
## LIFE IS *"A VIRTUE"*

The unexamined *life* is not worth living.
*(Socrates)*

2.  *T*rue virtue is *life* under the direction of reason.
*(Spinoza)*

3.  *W*hen Agesilaus the Great was asked: "How is it that Sparta is not surrounded by walls?", he replied: "What makes a city strong is not timber and stone, but its citizens' virtues." *(***)*

4.  *V*irtue consists, not in abstaining from vice, but in not desiring it. **(George Bernard Shaw)**

5.  *T*he superior man thinks only of virtue; the common man thinks of comfort. **(Confucius)**

6.  *L*ive a good *life*. If there are gods and they are just, then they will not care how devout you have been, but will welcome you based on the virtues you have lived by. If there are gods, but unjust, then you should not want to worship them. If there are no gods, then you will be gone, but will have lived a noble *life* that will live on in the memories of your loved ones. I am not afraid. **(Marcus Aurelius)**

7.  *L*oving means to love that which is unlovable – or it is no virtue at all; forgiving means to pardon the unpardonable – or it is no virtue at all; and to hope means hoping when things are hopeless – or it is no virtue at all. **(Gilbert Keith Chesterton)**

8.  *K*eep love in your heart. A *life* without it is like a sunless garden when the flowers are dead. The consciousness of loving and being loved brings a warmth and richness to *life* that nothing else can bring **(Oscar Wilde)**

9.  *N*othing in *life* can take the place of faithfulness and dependability. It is one of the greatest virtues. Brilliance, genius, competence – all are subservient to the quality of faithfulness. **(Wallace Fridy)**

10. *H*e who is virtuous is wise; and he who is wise is good; and he who is good is happy. **(***)**

11. *It* is good to commit the golden rule to memory but far better to commit it to *life.*               *(***)*

12. *Love life* and *life* will love you back. Love people and they will love you back.     *(Arthur Rubinstein)*

13. *The life* that goes out in love to all is the *life* that is full, and rich, and continually expanding in beauty and in power.                  *(R. W Trine)*

14. *All* things work together for good to those who love God and are called according to His purpose.
*(Romans 8:28)*

15. *Develop* an attitude of gratitude, and give thanks for everything that happens to you, knowing that every step forward is a step toward achieving something bigger and better than your current situation.                  *(Brian Tracey)*

16. *Gratitude* is not only the greatest of virtues, but the parent of all the others.                  *(Cicero)*

17. *How* far you go in *life* depends on your being tender with the young, compassionate with the aged, sympathetic with the striving, and tolerant of the weak and strong. Because some day in *life* you will have been all of these.
*(George Washington Carver)*

18. *Hope* is both the earliest and the most indispensable virtue inherent in the state of being alive. If *life* is to be sustained, hope must remain,

even where confidence is wounded, trust impaired.
**(Erik H. Erikson)**

19. *H*ope is the most significant fact of *life*. It provides human beings with a sense of destination and the energy to get started.     **(Norman Cousins)**

20. *I*f you wish success in *life*, make perseverance your bosom friend, experience your wise counselor, caution your elder brother, and hope your guardian genius.     **(Joseph Addison)**

21. *W*hatever happens, do not lose hold of the two main ropes of *life* - hope and faith.     **(***)**

20. *V*irtue, morality, and religion. This is the amour, my friend, and this alone that renders us invincible. These are the tactics we should study. If we lose these, we are conquered, fallen indeed.

**(Patrick Henry)**

23. *W*atch the way you live! It may be the only Bible someone has to read.     **(***)**

24. *Be* true to the best you know. This is your high ideal. If you do your best, you cannot do more.

**(H.W. Dresser)**

25. *Be* such a man, and live such a *life*, that if every man were such as you, and every *life* such as yours, this earth would be God's     paradise.

**(Phillips Brooks)**

26. *W*hat can I do?
I can talk out when others are silent.

I can say man when others say money.
I can stay up when others are asleep.
I can keep working when others have stopped to play.
I can give *life* big meaning when others give *life* little meaning.
I can say love when others say hate.
I can say every man when others say one man.
I can give myself to *life* when others refuse themselves to *life*.                     *(Horace Traubel)*

27. **W**atch your can'ts and can's.

If you would have some worthwhile plans, you've got to watch your can'ts and can's.

You can't aim low and then rise high; you can't succeed if you don't try;

You can't go wrong and come out right; you can't love sin and walk in light;

You can't throw time and means away and live sublime from day to day.

You can be great if you'll be good and do God's will as men should.

You can ascend as men should. You can ascend **life**'s upward road, although you bear a heavy load. You can be honest, truthful and clean, by turning from the low and mean; by words and deed, or by your pen. So watch your can'ts and watch your can's and watch your walk and watch your stands and watch the way you talk and act and do not take the false for fact; and watch the things that mar or make; for *life* is great to every man who lives to do the best he can. *(***)*

28. *T*he shortest and surest way to live with honor in the world is to be in reality what we would appear to be; and if we observe, we shall find that all human virtues increase and strengthen themselves by the practice and experience of them. *(Socrates)*

29. *A* handful of good *life* is better than a bushel of learning. *(***)*

30. *W*hatever you are, be a good one.
*(Abraham Lincoln)*

31. *I*f I can stop one heart from breaking, I shall not live in vain. If I can ease one *life* the aching, or cool one pain, or help one fainting robin unto his nest again, I shall not live in vain. If I can show a spark of light to someone wandering in darkness, I shall not live in vain. *(Emily Dickson)*

32. *I* feel the capacity to care is the thing which gives **life** its deepest significance. *(Pablo Casals)*

33. *C*onstant kindness can accomplish much. As the sun makes ice melt, kindness causes misunderstanding, mistrust, and hostility to evaporate. *(Albert Schweitzer)*

34. *A* good temper is not only a business asset. It is the secret of health. The longer you live, the more you will learn that a disordered temper produces a disordered body. *(B.C. Forbes)*

35. **N**o matter how you feel or what is disturbing your peace of mind, never allow yourself to send out a discouraging, a cruel or an unkind word or thought. **(O.S. Marden)**

36. **H**umility is one of the most important qualities which you must have because if you are humble, if you realize that you are no threat to them, then people will embrace you, they will listen to you. **(Nelson Mandela)**

37. **O**nly people who possess firmness can possess true gentleness. **(La Rochefoucauld)**

38. **C**onquer a man who never gives, by gifts; subdue untruthful men by truthfulness; vanquish an angry man by gentleness; and overcome the evil man by goodness. **(Mahabharata)**

39. **W**e make a living by what we get; we make a *life* by what we give. **(Winston Churchill)**

40. **T**he best thing to give your enemy is forgiveness; to an opponent tolerance; to a friend your heart; to a child a good example; to your father deference; to your mother conduct that will make her proud of you; to yourself, respect; to all men charity. **(Arthur James Balfur)**

41. **H**e who has not forgiven an enemy has not yet tasted one of the most sublime enjoyments of *life*. **(Johann K. Lavater)**

42. **B**e not overcome by evil, but overcome evil with good. **(Paul of Tarsus in Rom. 12:21)**

43. **G**oodness is the only investment that never fails. **(Henry David Thoreau)**

44. **T**he worst evil lies not in committing crimes but in neglecting the good we can do. **(Leon Bloy)**

45. **R**eturning good for evil is the noblest form of virtue. **(***)**

46. **T**he best way to escape evil is to pursue good. **(John Mason)**

47. **L**ook for strength in people, not weakness; good, not evil. Most of us find what we search for. **(J. Wilbur Chapman)**

48. **Life** is like a magic vase filled to the brim. When you dip into it or draw from it, it overflows into the hands of those who drop treasures into it. Drop in kindness and you will receive understanding. Drop in charity and you will receive love. Drop in hate and you will receive malice. Drop in envy and you will receive criticism. You alone control the treasures that **life** overflows into your heart and hands. You must watch carefully what you put into this magic vase. **(Phoenician Parable)**

49. **W**hen we live habitually with the wicked, we become necessarily their victims or their disciples; on the contrary, when we associate with the

virtuous, we form ourselves in imitation of their virtues, or at least lose, every day, something of our faults. **(Agapetus I)**

50. **D**o all the good you can,
    By all the means you can,
    In all the ways you can,
    In all the places you can,
    At all the times you can,
    To all the people you can,
    As long as ever you can.

    **(John Wesley)**

51. **L**ives of great men all remind us we can make our lives sublime; and departing, leave behind us footprints on the sands of time. **(Henry Longfellow)**

52. **I** shall pass this way but once. Any good I can do or any evil I can undo, let me do it now.

    **(Stephen Gullet)**

53. **I** expect to pass through **life** but once. If therefore there be any kindness I can show or any good things I can do to my fellow being, let me do it now, and not defer or neglect it, as I shall not pass this way again. **(William Penn)**

54. **I** am not bound to win, but I am bound to be true. I am not bound to succeed, but I am bound to live by the light that I have. I must stand with anybody that stands right, and part with him when he goes wrong. **(Abraham Lincoln)**

55. *T*he end and perfection of our victories is to avoid the vices and infirmities of those whom we subdue. **(Alexander the Great)**

56. *P*eople with integrity are those whose words match their deeds and behaviors mirror their values. **(Stephen Covey)**

57. *L*ive *life* like the Good Samaritan who asked 'If I do not stop to help this man, what will happen to him?' rather than the priest or Leviathan who asked 'If I stop to help this man, what will happen to me?' You can ask this question in a million of situations. **(***)**

58. *I*t is important that with everyone, we are humble, patient, respectful, cordial, gracious and yielding in all things permissible. **(***)**

59. *Life* is a long lesson in humility. **(James M. Barrie)**

60. *The* most important quality for a human being to master is 'Equanimity'. **(Antonius Pracus)**

61. *N*ever believe anything bad about anybody unless you positively know it to be true; never tell even that unless you feel that it is absolutely necessary and that God is listening while you tell it. **(Henry Van Dyke)**

62. *H*ate no one, no matter how much they have wronged you. Live humbly no matter how wealthy you become.

Think positively, no matter how hard life gets. Give much, even if you have been given little. Forgive all, especially yourself, and never stop believing that the best is yet to come. **(***)**

63. *T*he greatest happiness of **life** is the conviction that we are loved. **(Victor Hugo)**

64. *H*appiness is the only sanction in *life*; where happiness fails, existence remains a mad and lamentable experiment. **(George Santayana)**

65. *N*othing great was ever achieved without enthusiasm **(Ralph Waldo Emerson)**

66. *E*xcellence can be attained if you …
Care more than others think is wise,
Risk more than others think is safe,
Dream more than others think is practical,
Expect more than others think is possible.
**(John Mason)**

67. *I* believe in one God and no more; and I hope for happiness beyond this *life*. I believe in the equality of man; and I believe that religious duties consist in doing justice, loving mercy, and endeavoring to make our fellow creatures happy. **(Thomas Paine)**

68. **A life** spent worthily is measured by deeds, not by years. **(Sheridan)**

69. *A*lways the higher a *life* is, the more it is beautiful in its place, and can be beautiful nowhere else.
**(Phillips Brooks)**

70. *Y*our kindness may be treated as your weakness...still be kind.

The good you do today will be forgotten tomorrow...still be good.

Your forthrightness may be treated as high-handedness insubordination...still be forthright.

Virtues and values of **life** may mean little for people...still be virtuous.

Your help to others may go unheeded and unnoticed...still be helpful.

If you are successful, you will win false friends and true enemies...still succeed.

Honesty and frankness make you vulnerable...still be frank and honest.

Your faith in God and love for humanity may be taken as orthodoxy and foolishness ...still have faith in God. **(***)**

71. *G*reatness is not found in possessions, power, position or prestige. It is discovered in goodness, humility, service & character. *(WA Ward)*

# CHAPTER TWELVE
## LIFE IS *"CONCERN FOR OTHERS"*

*L**ife*** is an exciting business and most exciting when it is lived for others.
*(Helen Keller)*

2.  *No* man has learned the meaning of *life* until he has surrendered his ego to the service of his fellow men.
*(Beran Wolfe)*

3.  *T*he most satisfying thing in *life* is to have been able to give a large part of oneself to others.
**(Pierre de Chartin)**

4.  *E*very day of my *life* I become more convinced that the surest way to reach the summits of *life* is to help other people reach their plateaus.
**(Zig Ziglar)**

5.  *T*he more you learn what to do with yourself, and the more you do for others, the more you will learn to enjoy the abundant *life*.
**(William Boetcker)**

6.  *W*hat do we live for, if it is not to make *life* less difficult for each other?  **(George Eliot)**

7.  *T*reat others with dignity and kindness even if they seem to be the "least".  **(***)**

8.  *O*nly a *life* lived for others is a *life* worthwhile.
**(Albert Einstein)**

9.  *U*nless *life* is lived for others, it is not worthwhile.
**(Mother Teresa)**

10. *L*ife is not measured by its duration, but by its donation.  **(Shakespeare)**

11. *W*e are born for cooperation, as the feet, the hands, the eyelids, and the upper and lower jaws.
**(Marcus Aurelius Antoninus)**

12. *T*he person who tries to live alone will not succeed as a human being. His heart withers if it does not

answer another heart. His mind shrinks away if he hears only the echoes of his own thoughts and finds no other inspiration. **(Pearl S. Buck)**

13. *T*here is a destiny which makes us brethren. None goes his way alone. All that we send into the lives of others comes back into our own.

**(Edward Markham)**

14. *Our life* is made up of relationships–relationship with our creator, with ourselves, with fellow humans and with our world.

The right relationship brings us peace, harmony and joy. **(Kaitholil)**

15. *Y*our daily *life* is your temple and your religion. Whenever you enter into it, take with you all. Take the plough and the forge and the mallet and the lute, the things you have fashioned in necessity or for delight. For in reverie you cannot rise above your achievements, nor fall lower than your failures. And take with you all men. For in adoration, you cannot fly higher than their hopes nor humble yourself lower than their despair.

**(Kahlil Gibran)**

16. *E*ach of us is here for a brief sojourn; for what purpose he knows not though he sometimes thinks he senses it. But without going deeper than our daily *life,* it is plain that we exist for our fellow-men–in the first place for those upon whose smiles and welfare our happiness depends, and next for those entire unknown to us personally but to whose destinies we are bound by the tie of

sympathy. A hundred times every day I remind myself that my inner and outer *life* depends on the labours of other men, living and dead, and that I must exert myself in order to give in the measure as I have received and am still receiving.

**(Albert Einstein)**

17. *N*o man has learned to live until he can rise above the narrow confines of his individualistic concerns, to the broader concern of all humanity. Length without breadth is like a self-contained tributary having no outward flow to the ocean. Stagnant, still and stale, it lacks both *life* and freshness. In order to live creatively and meaningfully, one's self-concern must be wedded to others' concerns.

**(Martin Luther King, Fr.)**

18. *I* am convinced that my *life* belongs to the whole community; and as long as I live, it is my privilege to do for it whatever I can, for the harder I work, the more I live. I rejoice in *life* for its own sake.

**(George Bernard Shaw)**

19. *I*t is impossible to overemphasize the immense need humans have: to be really listened to, to be taken seriously, and to be understood. No one can fully develop freely in this world and find a complete *life* without feeling understood by at least one person. **(***)**

20. *T*o be happy is easy enough if we forgive ourselves, forgive others, and live with thanksgiving. No self-centered people, no ungrateful soul can ever be happy, much less, make

anyone else happy. **Life** is giving, not getting.
*(Joseph Fort Newton)*

21. *T*he greatest mystery in **life** is that satisfaction is felt not by those who take and make demands but by those who give and make sacrifices. In them alone, the energy of **life** does not fail.
*(Nicolas Berdyaev)*

22. *A*ll the other pleasures of **life** seem to wear out, but the pleasure of helping others in distress never does. *(Julius Rosenwald)*

23. *O*bserve around you and be thankful for all that you have in this transitory lifetime.
    Enjoy life how it is and as it comes. Things are worse for others and a lot better for you. Complain less and give more. *(***)*

24. *P*eople who live for self never succeed in satisfying self or anybody else. *(Trumbull)*

25. *A*ny person who seeks only his own happiness and fulfillment will never find them. *(George Kaitholil)*

26. *T*he entire population of the universe, with one trifling exception, is composed of others.
*(John Andrew Holmes)*

27. *A*nything, everything, little or big, becomes an adventure when the right person shares it. Nothing, nothing, nothing is worthwhile when we have to do it all alone. *(Kathleen Norris)*

28. *A* good way to forget your own troubles is to help others out of theirs. When you share, you do not lessen, but increase your *life*.          *(John Mason)*

29. *T*hose who bring sunshine into the lives of others cannot keep it from themselves.  *(James M. Barrie)*

30. *I*t is one of the most beautiful compensations of *life*, that no one can sincerely try to help another without actually helping himself/herself.     *(***)*

31. *H*appiness is a by-product of an effort to make someone else happy.          *(Gretta Palmer)*

32. *I* slept and dreamt that *life* was nothing but joy; I awoke and saw that *life* was service; I served and I understood that service was joy.          *(Tagore)*

33. *I* am endeavouring to see God through service to humanity, for I know that God is neither in heaven, nor down below, but in everyone.
*(Mahatma Gandhi)*

34. *H*e that cannot forgive others breaks the bridge over which he must pass himself; for every man has need to be forgiven.          *(E. Herbert)*

35. *D*o unto others what you want them to do unto to you.          *(Mathew 7:12)*

36. *I*f your heart acquires strength, you will be able to remove blemishes from others without thinking evil of them.          *(Mohandas K. Gandhi)*

37. *I*nstead of pointing a critical finger, try holding out a helping hand. **(***)**

38. *A* truly great person is one, in whose presence others feel great. **(***)**

39. *I*f God has loved us, we must be loveable. If God has accepted us, we must be acceptable. If God has shared His *life* with us, we must also share our *life* with others. *Life* itself can't give you joy unless you really will it. *Life* just gives you time and space. It's up to you to fill it, so make the most of it. **(***)**

40. *W*hatever God does in your *life* is not so that you can keep it to yourself. He wants you to give to others. **(R. Browne)**

41. *A*dapt yourself to the things among which your lot has been cast and love sincerely the fellow creatures with whom destiny has ordained that you shall live. **(Marcus Aurelius)**

42. **D**o not withhold good from those whom it is due, when it is in your power to do it. **(***)**

43. **Life's Joy**: God gives us joy that we might give. He gives us love that we may share. Sometimes He gives us loads to lift that we may learn to bear. For *life* is gladder when we give, and love is sweeter when we share; and heavy loads rest lightly, too, when we have learned to bear. **(William Jay)**

44. **D**o not neglect to do good and to share what you have, for such sacrifices are pleasing to God.

**(Heb. 13:16)**

45. **D**o good to others. it will come back to you in unexpected ways

**(***)**

46. **R**esolve to enjoy **life** to the fullest each day dedicated to making others happy when you can, thus ensuring your own greater happing.

**(***)**

47. **I** sincerely believe that we are given **life** to enjoy and make it more enjoyable for others... The best way to do this is to get in the middle of it.

**(Henry L. Harrell)**

48. **O**ne of the secrets of a long and fruitful **life** is to forgive everybody everything every night before you go to bed.

**(Ann Landers)**

49. **I**n gratitude for your own good fortune, you must render in return some sacrifice of your **life** for other **life**.

**(Albert Schweitzer)**

50. **Life** is so short to spend your precious time trying to convince a person who wants to live in gloom and doom otherwise. Give lifting that person your best shot, but don't hang around long enough for his or her bad attitude to pull you down. Instead, surround yourself with optimistic people.

**(Zig Ziglar)**

51. **E**ffective ways to make others feel important:

   i. Use their name.

   ii. Express sincere gratitude.

   iii. Do more listening than talking.

    iv.  Talk more about them than about yourself.

    v.  Be authentically interested.

    vi.  Be sincere in your praise.

    vii. Show your care.       **(Roy T. Bennett)**

52. *S*mile at each other, smile at your wife, smile at your husband, smile at your children, and smile at each other. It doesn't matter who it is - and that will help you to grow up in greater love for each other.       **(Mother Teresa)**

# CHAPTER THIRTEEN
## LIFE IS *"TRUSTING IN GOD"*

**A** *life* centered around God is a *life* of completeness. **(Ellen G. White)**

2. *Y*ou must trust in God because he knows your name, thinks about you, fights for you, is always with you, has a plan for you, and is your refuge.

*(***)*

3.  *G*ive yourself to God. He can do more with you than you can. **(***)**

4.  *T*rust in yourself and you are doomed to disappointment; trust in your friends and they will die and leave you; trust in money and you may have it taken from you; trust in reputation and some slanderous tongue may blast it; but trust in God, and you are never to be confounded in time or eternity. **(Dwight L. Moody)**

5.  *I*n our ocean of **life**, God is our buoyant force, no matter how strong the wind and the gigantic the waves are anchored to him. **(***)**

6.  *E*very single one of us is handicapped– physically, mentally, socially, and spiritually– to some degree; and although we seldom think about it, the person without faith has a far greater handicap than the person without feet. **(Frank K. Ellis)**

7.  *T*rust God for great things; with your five loaves and two fishes, He will show you a way to feed thousands. **(Horace Bushnell)**

8.  *F*ill your **life** with the word of God and strong faith will be produced. **(Trevor Newport)**

9.  *W*henever you are in doubt, faith it. **(***)**

10. **Life** without faith in something is too narrow of space in which to live. **(George Spaulding)**

11. *A*ll I have seen teaches me to trust the Creator for all I have not seen. **(Ralph Waldo Emerson)**

12. **A**t my lowest:  God is my hope.
    At my Darkest: God is my light.
    At my weakest: God is my strength.
    At my saddest: God is my Comforter.        **(***)**

13. **L**ive, as it were, on trust; all that is in you, all that you are, is only loaned to you; make use of it according to the will of Him who lends it, but never regard it for a moment as your own.

    **(Fenelon)**

14. **G**od will make a way for you if you'll give Him full control.  Trust Him with your **life** and hopes and He'll help you reach your goal. Sing a little song of faith, keep your courage bright, and soon you'll see that God has turned your darkness into light.

    **(Rachel Hartnett)**

15. **G**od always has something for you: A key for every problem, a light for every shadow, a relief for every sorrow, and a plan for every tomorrow.        **(***)**

16. **M**an has so many imperfections, defects, errors, insufficiencies and doubts in his way of going about things. It becomes necessary to put everything in the hands of Divine Mercy and let ourselves be guided. Never force the hand of Prudence.        **(James Alberione)**

17. **S**pread out your petition before God and then say, 'Thy will, not mine, be done.' The sweetest lesson I have learned in God's school is to let the Lord choose for me.        **(Dwight L. Moody)**

18. **G**od cannot be used as a stop-gap. We must not wait until we are at the end of our tether. He must be found at the centre of **life**, and not only in death, in health and in vigor; and not only in suffering, in activity, and not only in sin.

**(Dietrich Bonhoeffer)**

19. **If** you want a brief and efficacious method, which at the same time embraces all the other methods, to overcome any temptations and trials, and to acquire perfection, it is living in the presence of God. **(St. Basil)**

20. **T**he way you fell today has little to do with what God is actually doing in your **life**. He's working behind the scenes whether you realise it or not! Be stable-minded by focusing your thoughts on his word so that you can confidently embrace the good plans he has for you. **(James 1:6)**

21. **Y**ou will be what the Lord has destined you to be by His Grace even if you persist and persist. L have for you, plans to prosper you and not to harm you, plans to give hope and a future.

**(Jeremiah 29:11)**

22. **W**hatever **life** shall bring your way, Through each and every fleeting day, Throughout the months and long years, too, God in His heaven shall care for you. **(***)**

23. **N**ever forget that you are not alone. The divine is with you, helping and guiding. He is the companion who never fails, the friend whose love

comforts and strengthens. Have faith and He will do everything for you. *(Aurobindo)*

24. *T*rust men, and they will be true to you; treat them greatly and they will show themselves great.
*(Ralph Waldo Emerson)*

25. *T*he person who often looks up to God rarely looks down on any man. *(***)*

26. *G*et into the habit of dealing with God about everything. Unless in the first waking moment of the day you learn to fling the door wide back and let God in, you will work on a wrong level all day; but swing the door wide open and pray to your Father in secret, and every public thing will be stamped with the presence of God.
*(Oswald Chamber)*

# CHAPTER FOURTEEN
## LIFE IS *"CHEERFULNESS"*

Cheerfulness is the great lubricant of the wheels of *life*. It lightens labour, diminishes difficulties, and mitigates misfortunes. Cheerfulness gives creative power which pessimism never possesses. A sunny, hopeful, optimistic disposition sweetens *life*, lightens its inevitable drudgery, and eases the jolts along the road. *(Councilor)*

2.  Cheerfulness costs nothing; yet is beyond price. It is an asset for both business and body. The big men of today, the leaders of tomorrow are those who can blend cheerfulness with their brains.

*(B.C. Forbes)*

3.  ***T***he men who I have seen succeed best in ***life***, have always been cheerful and hopeful men, who went about their business with smiles on their faces, and took the challenges and chances of this mortal ***life*** like men, facing rough and smooth alike as it came.                    ***(Charles Kingsley)***

4.  ***A*** smile on your lips: cheers your heart, keeps you in good humour, preserves peace in your soul, promotes your health, beautifies your face, induces kindly thoughts, and inspires kindly deeds.      ***(***)***

5.  ***T***he thing that goes the furthest towards making ***life*** worthwhile, that costs the least, and does the most, is just a pleasant smile.                 ***(***)***

6.  ***O***f all the things you wear, your expression is the most important.                          ***(Janet Lanyne)***

7.  ***S***mile-Smiling More Increases ***Life*** Expectancy.
                                    ***(Robert Seymour)***

8.  ***A*** warm smile is the universal language of kindness.                               ***(WA Ward)***

9.  ***E***very man who expects to receive happiness is obligated to give happiness.            ***(John Mason)***

10. ***C***heerfulness means a contented spirit, a pure heart, a kind and loving disposition; it means humility and charity, a generous appreciation of others, and a modest opinion of self.
                        ***(William Makepeace Thackeray)***

11. **W**ondrous is the strength of cheerfulness, and its power of endurance – the cheerful man will do more in the same time, will do it better, will persevere in it longer than the sad or sullen.

*(Thomas Carlyle)*

12. **T**he best way to cheer yourself up is to try to cheer somebody else up. *(Mark Twain)*

13. **Life** is like a mirror: we get the best results when we smile at it. *(Proverb)*

14. **A** sense of humour is the lubricant of **life**'s machinery. *(Proverb)*

15. **H**umour is to **life** what shock absorbers are to automobiles. *(Stan Toler)*

16. **L**earn to laugh. And most of all, learn to laugh at yourself. The person, who can give a riotous account of his own *faux pas*, will never have to listen to another's embarrassing account of it. He will rarely know the sting of humiliation. He is a delight to be with; but more important, he is enjoying his own **life**, and applying to his ills and errors the most soothing balm the human spirit has devised – laughter. *(Margaret M. Butts)*

17. **S**hared laughter creates a bond of friendship. When people laugh together, they cease to be young and old, master and pupils, worker and driver. They have become a single group of human beings, enjoying their existence. *(W. Grant Lee)*

18. The way you look on the outside is considered to be an expression of the kind of person you are on the inside. **(Brian Tracey)**

19. *Laughter* is the shock absorber that eases the blows of *life*. **(***)**

20. *Laughter* is the best medicine for a long and happy *life*. He who laughs—lasts. **(***)**

21. *You* have not fulfilled every duty, unless you have fulfilled that of being cheerful and kind. **(C. Buxton)**

# CHAPTER FIFTEEN
## LIFE IS *"ENJOYING FRIENDSHIP"*

**F**riendship is one of the sweetest joys of *life*. Many might have failed beneath the bitterness of their trial had they not found a friend. ***(Charles H. Spurgeon)***

2.  **W**ise is the person who fortifies his life with the right friendships. If you ran with wolves, you will learn how to howl. But, if you associate with eagles, you will learn how to soar to great heights. A mirror reflects a man's face, but what he is really like is shown by the kind of friends he chooses.

    *(***)*

3.  *F*riendship multiplies the good of *life* and divides the evil. **(Balthazar Gracian)**

4.  *F*riendship is the inexpressible comfort of feeling safe with a person, having neither to weigh thoughts nor measure words. **(George Eliot)**

5.  *W*hat is a friend? A single soul dwelling in two bodies. **(Aristotle)**

6.  *F*riendship is among the better gifts that we can possess in this world. **(Savonarola)**

7.  *A* friend may well be reckoned the masterpiece of nature. **(Ralph Waldo Emerson)**

8.  *Y*our friend is the man who knows all about you, and still likes you. **(Elbert Hubbard)**

9.  *A* true friend sees beyond you to what you can be. **(John Mason)**

10. *M*y best friend is the man who in wishing me well, wishes it for my sake. **(Aristotle)**

11. *A* friend can tell you things you don't want to tell yourself. **(Francis Ward Welter)**

12. *T*rue friendship is like sound health; the value of it is seldom known until it be lost. **(Charles Caleb Colton)**

13. *T*here are moments in our lives so lovely, they transcend earth, and anticipate heaven for us. This

foretaste of eternity has made it clear to me the perpetual and all–embracing service that friendship should ever be. **(Helen Keller)**

14. **F**riends are those rare people who ask how we are, and then wait to hear the answer.

    **(Ed Cunningham)**

15. **L**et your friends come into your **life**; let them see you as you are, and not find you trying to be somebody else. **(Emma Whitcomb Babcock)**

16. **T**reat your friends as you do your pictures, and place them in their best light.

    **(Jennie Jerome Churchill)**

17. **N**ever explain yourself:
    Your friends don't need it and your enemies won't believe it. **(***)**

18. **I** value the friend who for me finds time on his calendar, but I cherish the friend who for me does not consult his calendar. **(Robert Brault)**

19. **T**o let friendship, die away by negligence and silence is certainly not wise. It is voluntarily to throw away one of the greatest comforts of this weary pilgrimage. **(Samuel Johnson)**

20. **F**riends contribute materially towards your education. You derive most of your knowledge of getting on with people from friends who are sufficiently interested and patient to tell you what they know. It is only from a friend you will listen

to a disagreeable truth about yourself. In any way you wish to look at the subject, a friend is an important asset. **(Charles Gow)**

21. **A** friend is a person who thinks you're a good egg even though you're slightly cracked. **(***)**

22. **A** friend will joyfully sing with you when you are on the mountain top and silently walk beside you are in the valley. **(***)**

23. **A** loyal friend laughs at your jokes when they're not so good, and sympathizes with your problems when they're not so bad. **(Arnold H. Glasow)**

24. **I**t takes a great soul to be a true friend. One must forgive much, forget much, and forbear much.
**(Anna Robertson Brown)**

25. **I** went out to seek a friend,
But could not find one there.
I went out to be a friend,
And friends were everywhere. **(Kathleen A. Kelly)**

26. **S**ome people come into our lives and quickly go. Some stay for a while and leave footprints on our hearts, and we are never ever the same.
**(Flavia Weedn)**

27. **B**e courteous to all, but intimate with few, and let those few be well tried before you give them your confidence. True friendship is a plant of slow growth, and must undergo and withstand the

shocks of adversity before it is entitled to the appellation. *(***)*

28. **W**e cannot tell the precise moment when friendship is formed. As in filling a vessel drop by drop, there is at last a drop which makes it run over; so, in a sense of kindnesses there is at last one which makes the heart run over.

**(James Boswen)**

29. **F**riends are God's way of taking care of us. *(***)*

30. **F**riends last longer the less they are used. *(***)*

31. **H**e who has a thousand friends has not a friend to spare. **(Ralph Waldo Emerson)**

32. **T**hey that thrive well take counsel of their friends.
**(Shakespeare)**

33. **M**y best friend is the one that brings out the best in me. **(Henry Ford)**

34. **G**ood friends care for each other, close friends understand each other, but true friends Stay forever ... Beyond words, Beyond distance, Beyond time. *(***)*

35. **E**ncouragement is perhaps one of the greatest gift friends can ever give. An encouraging friend is a *life*line to steady a floundering heart, to bring sunshine to a cloudy day, and to deliver a blessing just looking for a place to land. **(Susan Duke)**

36. *I* count myself nothing else so happy as in a soul remembering my good friends. **(Shakespeare)**

37. *My* best friends are those who understand my past, believe in my future and accept me today as I am.
**(***)**

38. *G*ood friends, good books and a sleepy conscience: this is the ideal *life*. **(Mark Twain)**

39. *F*riendship is a happy thing, it makes us laugh, it makes us sing, it makes us take, it makes us give, above all else, it makes us live. **(A.J. Nimeth)**

40. *T*he greatest advantage of good friendship is that a person can thereby save himself from going the wrong way. **(Charles Menezes)**

41. *H*ow one handles his grief is a personal matter. Let the one who has suffered the loss take the lead. If he feels like talking, encourage him to talk. If he prefers to sit in silence, don't intrude on his silence. Friends should call, bring food, offer to run errands, and do what needs to be done. A hug, a squeeze of the hand, a look which says, "I am here, if you need me", conveys more than a thousand words. **(Abigail Van Buren)**

42. *F*riendship with oneself is all important, because without it one cannot be friends with anyone else in the world.
**(Eleanor Roosevelt)**

43. *R*adiate friendship and it will be returned tenfold.
**(Henry P. David)**

# CHAPTER SIXTEEN
## LIFE IS *"ENJOYING RECREATION"*

Vacations are times to spend re-creating the energies of *life* – physical, mental, emotional, and spiritual. In a busy workaday world, too often the vital areas of *life* are neglected and spent. Vacation time should be an opportunity to check out the energy levels of *life* and to replenish the low ones. Every person needs a period away from the toil and routine. He needs a time to replenish his mental energies, regroup his physical powers, reconsider his emotional needs, and review his spiritual progress.   **(*C. Neil Strait*)**

2.  *Life* lived amidst tension and busyness needs leisure – leisure that re-creates and renews. Leisure

should be a time to think new thoughts, not ponder old ills. **(C. Neil Strait)**

3. *L*eisure consist<u>s</u> in all those virtuous activities by which a man grows morally, intellectually, and spiritually. It is that which makes a life worth living. **(Cicero)**

4. *Life* must be lived as play. **(Plato)**

5. *L*ive and work but do not forget to play, to have fun in *life* and really enjoy it. **(Eileen Caddy)**

6. **W**hen we are full of **life**, when each sense overflows with vitality, then we became prodigal, we scatter ourselves broadest, we take chances, risk great odds, love, laugh, dance, write poems, paint pictures, roam with children; in short, we play. It is only the impotent who do not play. The people who play are the creators. **(Holbrook Jackson)**

7. *L*eisure is time for doing something useful. **(Benjamin Franklin)**

8. *L*eisure time should be an occasion for deep purpose to throb and for ideas to ferment. Where a man allows leisure to slip without some creative use, he has forfeited a bit of happiness. **(C. Neil Strait)**

9. *T*o be able to fill leisure intelligently is the last product of civilization, and at present very few people have reached that level. **(Bertrand Russell)**

10. **W**e do not rest because our work is done; we rest because God commanded it and created us to have a need for it. **(Gordon MacDonald)**

11. **R**est has cured more people than all the medicine in the world. **(Harold J. Reilly)**

12. Take rest; a field that has rested gives a bountiful crop. **(Ovid)**

13. **Life** itself still remains a very effective therapist. **(Karen Horney)**

14. **S**unshine is delicious, rain is refreshing, wind braces up, and snow is exhilarating; there is no such thing as bad weather, only different kinds of weather. **(John Ruskin)**

15. **H**ome is where you live your **life** and build your memories. **(***)**

# CHAPTER SEVENTEEN
## LIFE IS *"ENJOYING LITTLE ACTS"*

**L**earn to enjoy the little things – God made so many of them. *(***)*

2.  *I*n the game of **life**, it's not the major things which often determine success or failure, happiness or misery – it's the little things. *(Zig Ziglar)*

3.  *M*ost of the critical things in **life**, which become the starting points of human destiny, are little things. *(R. Smith)*

4.  *D*o little things as though they were great, because of the majesty of Jesus Christ who docs them in us, and who lives our *life*; and do the greatest things as though they were little and easy, because of His omnipotence.          **(Blaise Pascal)**

5.  *Life* is not lost by dying; *life* is lost minute by minute, day by dragging day, in all the thousand small uncaring ways.          **(Stephen Vincent Benet)**

6.  *T*he constant interchange of those thousand little courtesies which imperceptibly sweeten *life* has a happy effect upon the features and spreads a mellow evening charm over the wrinkles of old a
          (*Washington Irving*)

7.  *M*ost of *life* is made up of little things.
          *(John M. Drescher)*

8.  *T*he best portion of a good man's *life* is his little, nameless, unremembered acts of kindness and of love.          (*William Wordsworth*)

9.  *I*f you have not often felt the joy of doing a kind act, you have neglected much - and most of all, yourself.          **(A. Nielsen)**

10. *I* do not believe that a person who ignores the small things of *life*, the small truths, the small decencies, the small pleasantness, the small graciousness, can undertake anything in a big way.
          (*Jawaharlal Nehru*)

11. **N**o act of kindness, no matter how small is ever wasted. **(Aesop)**

12. **T**he most decisive actions of our **life** …are most often unconsidered action. **(Andre Gide)**

13. **T**he most rewarding things you do in **life** are often the ones that look like they cannot be done. **(Arnold Palmer)**

14. **I** long to accomplish a great and noble task, but it is my chief duty to accomplish humble tasks as though they were great and noble. The world is moved along, not only by the mighty shoves of its heroes, but also by the aggregate of the tiny pushes of each honest worker. **(Helen Keller)**

15. **Life** consists not in holding good cards but in playing those you hold well. **(Josh Billings)**

16. **T**he grand essentials to happiness in this **life** are: something to do; something to love; and something to hope for. **(Joseph Addison)**

17. **A**ll great achievements have been characterized by extreme care, infinite painstaking, even to the minutest detail. **(Elbert Hubbard)**

18. **T**he crowning fortune of a man is to be born to some pursuit which finds him employment and happiness, whether it be to make baskets, or broadswords, or canals, or statues, or songs. **(Ralph Waldo Emerson)**

19. *It* does not take great men to do great things; it only takes consecrated men. **(*Phillips Brooks*)**

20. *We* sow a thought and reap an act. We sow an act and reap a habit. We sow a habit and reap a character. We sow a character and reap a destiny.
**(*William M. Thackery*)**

21. *Life* is so short, but there is always time enough for courtesy. **(*Ralph Waldo Emerson*)**

22. *Is* not *life* a hundred times too short for us to bore ourselves? **(*Friedrich Nietzsche)*

# CHAPTER EIGHTEEN
## LIFE IS *"FOLLOWING RULES"*

*I*n the game of *life*, if you break the rules, the rules will eventually break you. Live by the golden rule! *(***)*

2.  **W**e get out of *life* as much as we put into it. *(***)*

3.  **R**esolved:

    ☐ to live with all my might while I do live.

    ☐ never to lose one moment of time, to improve it in the most profitable way I possibly can.

    ☐ never to do anything that I should despise or think meanly of in another.

☐ never to do anything out of revenge.

☐ never to do anything that I should be afraid to do if it were the last hour of my *life*.

*(Jonathan Edwards)*

4. *M*ake it a rule of *life* never to regret and never to look back. Regret is an appalling waste of energy. You can't build on it. It's only good for wallowing in. **(Katherine Mansfield)**

5. *Life* is like a boomerang; you always get back what you send out. **(Robert Seymour)**

6. *A*s a rule, he or she who has the most information will have the greatest success in *life*.

**(Benjamin Disraeli)**

7. *I*f you speak words of love, people will react to you with love. **(Steve Brow)**

8. *Life* is like a mirror. If you smile at it, it will smile at you. If you frown at it, it will frown at you.

**(***)**

9. *T*o change your *life*, change your choices and the use of your words. **(Edwin Louis Cole)**

10. *Y*ou know much if you know how to live.

**(Proverb)**

11. *N*ever put off till tomorrow what you can do today.
Never trouble another for what you can do yourself.
Never spend your money before you have it.

Never buy what you do not want because it is
cheap.
Pride costs us more than hunger, thirst and cold.
We seldom repent having eaten too little.
Nothing is troublesome that we do willingly.
How much pain the evils have caused us that have
never happened! Take things always by the smooth
handle. *(***)*

12. *M*ake decisions quickly. Be independent.
Act and stand firmly. Always have a fight on.
Learn to make news. Form alliances with other
leaders.
Consider defeats as lessons. Wall against danger.
Create a staff. Represent your following.
Reward loyalty. Have a great, worthy purpose.
*(***)*

13. *S*ix Rules to Live by:
Live as though you are a part of everyone.
Help everyone.
Do not let anyone feel alone. Love everyone.
Forgive everyone. Live like you are one with
everyone and everyone is one with God.
*(Harold Sherman)*

14. *F*ive Cardinal Rules for *Life*:

☐ Make peace with your past so it won't disturb
your present.

☐ What other people think of you, is none of your
business.

☐ Time heals almost everything. Give it time.

☐ No one is in charge of your happiness.  Except you.

☐ Don't compare your *life* to others and  don't judge them. You have no idea what their journey is all about.                    *(***)*

15. **Preventive Health Measures:**
    ☐ Drink purified or boiled clean water.

    ☐ Keep your clothes clean and neat.

    ☐ Live in a clean and well-ventilated environment.

    ☐ Protect yourself from mosquitoes.

    ☐ Eat more of fruits, vegetables and beans in your food varieties.

    ☐ Do physical exercises.

    ☐ Sleep well.                    *(Robert William)*

16. *T*he best things in *life* are nearest: Breath in your nostrils, light in your eyes, flowers at your feet, duties at your hand, the path of right just before you. Then do not gasp at the stars, but do *life*'s plain, common work as it comes, certain that daily duties and daily bread are the sweetest things in *life*.                    *(Robert Louis Stevenson)*

17. *A*lways carry yourself as though everyone is watching, even when no one is watching.
                    *(Brian Tracey)*

18. *T*o become childlike:
    ☐ Uncomplicate your *life* - be open and honest.

☐ Don't be afraid to admit, "I can't do that" or "I don't know."

☐ Don't hide your feelings or be afraid to show affection.

☐ Delight in simple things. Enjoy being you is expected of you.

☐ Don't hold grudges; let the past be past.

**(Thomas Finch)**

19. **A** healthy mind in a healthy body. God is **life**! Don't kill the body - not even by excess play or work. Do not diminish your strength and talents by imprudence or neglect. Strive rather to develop those in yourself with good educational methods. Develop your skills, improve the way you do your job, and enlarge your knowledge and your spheres of action. For the sake of yourself and those around you, develop your personality, being mindful of the truth and not appearances.

**(James Alberione)**

20. ☐ **Do** good to everyone.

☐ Speak ill of no one.

☐ Reflect before deciding.

☐ Do not speak while excited.

☐ Help the unfortunate.

☐ Admit your errors.

☐ Be patient with all.

☐ Do not listen to tale-bearers.

    ☐ Mistrust unkind reports.

    ☐ Prepare to die. *(***)*

21. *A*lways tell the truth and you never have to remember what you said. ***(T.L. Osborn)***

22. ***Emotional Maturity:***

    ☐ The ability to deal constructively with reality;
    ☐ The capacity to adapt to change;
    ☐ A relative freedom from symptoms that are produced by tensions and anxieties;
    ☐ The capacity to find more satisfaction from giving than receiving;
    ☐ The capacity to relate to other people in a consistent manner with mutual satisfaction and helpfulness;
    ☐ The capacity to sublimate, to direct one's instinctive hostile energy into creative and constructive outlets;
    ☐ The capacity to love. ***(William Menninger)***

23. *E*verything should be made as simple as possible, but not simpler. ***(Albert Einstein)***

24. *I*f you wish to develop your psychic faculties:

    ☐ Avoid discord of any kind.

    ☐ Positively do not let it appear in your home.

    ☐ Be helpful, cheerful, happy, and thoughtful of each other.

☐ Do not indulge the flesh in any excesses anything and everything in moderation is all right.

☐ Guard your emotions. Beware of anger, hate, jealousy, or worry of any kind.

☐ Anticipate good – look expectantly for good.

☐ Fill yourself with **LOVE**. Do not permit constipation – drink much water.

☐ Things will normally happen in their own time.

☐ Be casual and relaxed.

☐ Keep your thoughts and aspirations to yourself.

☐ Be not weary of well-doing.  (**Harold Sherman**)

25. ***Twelve things to remember:***
☐ The value of time,
☐ The success of perseverance,
☐ The pleasure of working,
☐ The dignity of simplicity,
☐ The worth of character,
☐ The power of kindness,
☐ The influence of example,
☐ The obligation of duty,
☐ The wisdom of economy,
☐ The virtue of patience,
☐ The improvement of talents.
☐ The joy of originating.  (**Marshall Field**)

26. **N**onviolence is the supreme law of *life*.
(***Indian Proverb***)

27. *T*he first rule for happiness is: avoid lengthy thinking on the past. Nothing is as far away as one hour ago. **(John Mason)**

28. **The six mistakes of man:**

   - ☐ The delusion that personal gain is made by crushing others.

   - ☐ The tendency to worry about things that cannot be changed or corrected.

   - ☐ Insisting that a thing is impossible because we cannot accomplish it.

   - ☐ Refusing to set aside trivial preferences.

   - ☐ Neglecting development and refinement of the mind, and not acquiring the habit of reading and studying.

   - ☐ Attempting to compel others to believe and live as we do. **(Cicero)**

29. *E*verything you now do is something you have chosen to do.

   Some people don't want to believe that. But if you're over age twenty-one, your *life* is what you're making of it. To change your *life*, you need to change your priorities. **(John C. Maxwell)**

30. ***Boy Scout Motto:***
"Be prepared."
And with it, the five Ps: "Proper Planning Prevents Poor Performance." *(***)*

31. ***B***y your own soul learn to live.
If men thwart you, take no heed.
If men hate you, have not a care.
Sing your song, dream your dream, and pray your prayer. *(***)*

32. ***Goals and the formula:***

First, identify what you want.
Second, clearly spell out why you want to reach that particular goal.
Third, list the obstacles that stand between you and your goal.
Fourth, identify the growth process – the things you need to know in order to get to your goal.
Fifth, identify the people you need to work with to reach your goal.
Sixth, develop a detailed plan of action to reach success.

Seventh, set a date on when you expect to reach that goal. *(Zig Ziglar)*

# CHAPTER NINETEEN
## LIFE IS *"A PURPOSE"*

**E**very man's *life* is a plan of God.
*(Horace Bushnell)*

2.  *M*any are the plans in a person's heart, but it is the Lord's purpose that prevails. *(Proverbs 19:21)*

3.  *I* am part of God, and God has a great purpose in life for me which He is revealing day by day as I grow in strength of body, mind, and spirit.

    **(Harold Sherman)**

4.  *T*he whole duty of man is summed up in obedience to God's will.

    **(George Washington Carver)**

5.  *T*he vision that you glorify in your mind, the ideal that you enthrone in your heart – this, you will build your *life* by, this you will become.

    **(James Lane Allen)**

6.  *P*eople ask me; what is the purpose of *life*? And I respond: In a nutshell, *life* is a preparation for eternity.

    **(Rick Warren)**

7.  *T*he ultimate aim or purpose of human *life* is to achieve happiness.

    **(Theodore Roosevelt)**

8.  *T*he purpose of human *life* is to serve, and to show compassion and the will to help others.

    **(Albert Schweitzer)**

9.  *O*ur prime purpose in this *life* is to help others. And if you can't help them, at least don't hurt them.

    **(Dalai Lama)**

10. *T*he purpose of our lives is to create something unique that entertains, instructs, challenges, or helps others.

    **(***)**

11. *W*ithout God, *life* has no purpose, and without purpose, *life* has no meaning. Without meaning, *life* has no significance or hope.      *(Rick Warren)*

12. *T*he purpose of *life* is to live a *life* of purpose.
    *(Robert Byrne)*

13. *Y*ou're not truly free until you've been made captive by your supreme mission in *life*.
    *(John Mason)*

14. *T*he great end of *life* is not knowledge but action.
    *(Thomas H. Huxley)*

15. *T*here is great meaning in *life* for those who are willing to journey.      *(Jim England)*

16. *O*ur business in *life* is not to get ahead of others, but to get ahead of ourselves – to break our own records, to outstrip our yesterdays by today, to do our work with more force than ever before.
    *(Stewart Johnson)*

17. *T*he ultimate purpose of all human action is the achievement      *(Aristotle)*

18. *T*hey're basically moments in which you're in touch with the meaning of *life*, when your relationship to the rest of the universe makes sense.      *(Barbara De Angelis)*

19. *W*e can discover the meaning in *life* in three different ways: first, by doing a deed; second, by experiencing a value; and third, by suffering.
    *(Victor Frank 1)*

20. *T*he goal of **life** is living in agreement with nature.
**(Zeno)**

21. *H*ave reverence for God, and obey his commands, because this is all that we were created for.
**(Eccl. 12:13)**

22. *T*he purpose of my **life** is to make me what the Almighty wants me to be. Then, I shall not measure things by their capacity to delight and please my tastes, ambitions, desires, and senses ... but only by their power to mould me in His likeness.
**(Robert D. Foster)**

23. *T*he greatest use of a **life** is to spend it for something that outlasts it.
**(William James)**

24. *A* man may fulfill the object of his existence by asking a question he cannot answer, and attempting a task he cannot achieve.
**(Oliver Wendell Holmes)**

25. *P*romise yourself to live your **life** as a revolution and not just a process of evolution.
**(Anthony J. D'Angelo)**

26. *T*he person who has no direction is a slave of his circumstances. The poorest person is not someone without money, but without purpose.
**(John Mason)**

27. *T*he greatest need of human beings is for a sense of meaning and purpose in **life**.
**(Victor Frank 1)**

28. *W*ithout a purpose, nothing should be done.
*(Marcus Aurelius)*

29. *W*hat is the meaning of *life?* To be happy and useful.
*(Tenzin Gyatso)*

30. *N*ever let someone else determine God's will for your *life.* No one else can understand God's unique call on your *life* as clearly as you.
*(Bob Briner and Ray Pritchard)*

31. *N*ever forget that the purpose for which a man lives is the improvement of the man himself, so that he may go out of this world having, in his great sphere or his small one, done some little good for his fellow creatures and labored a little to diminish the sin and sorrow that are in the world.
*(William E. Gladstone)*

32. *T*he best good you can do yourself is to identify your inborn gifts, abilities and talents and develop them for your *life.*
*(Robert William)*

33. *F*ind out what you really love to do, and then find a way to make a living doing it.
*(Napoleon Hill)*

34. *T*he potential for greatness lives within each of us.
*(John Maxwell)*

35. *O*ur plans miscarry because they have no aim. When a man does not know what harbor he is making for, no wind is the right wind.
*(Seneca)*

36. *E*very *life* should have a purpose to which it can give the energies of its mind and the enthusiasms

of its heart. That *life* without a purpose will be prey to the perverted ways waiting for the uncommitted *life*. **(C. Neil Strait)**

37. *Life* is for dreaming dreams, but few have the courage or will to realize them. **(Crenner Bradley)**

38. *W*ithout some goals and some efforts to reach them, no man can live. **(John Dewey)**

39. *I*f a man hasn't discovered something that he will die for, he isn't fit to live. **(Martin Luther King, Fr)**

40. *T*he purpose of *life* is to fight maturity. **(Dick Werthimer)**

41. *H*ave a purpose in *life,* and having it, throw into your work such strength of mind and muscle as God has given you. **(Thomas Carlyle)**

42. *Y*ou are the block. God is the sculptor. You cannot know what He is cutting you for and you never will in this *life*. All you want is patience, trust, confidence, and He does it all. **(Don John Chapman)**

43. *T*he purpose of *life* is not to be happy – but to matter, to be productive, to be useful, and to have it make some difference that you lived at **(Leo Roastan)**

44. *T*he first duty of a human being is to assume the right functional relationship to society – more

briefly, to find your real job, and do it.
**(Charlotte Perkins Gilman)**

45. *T*his is true joy of *life* - the being used up for a purpose recognized by yourself as a mighty one instead of being a feverish, selfish, little clod of ailments and grievances, complaining that the world will not devote itself to making you happy.
**(George Bernard Shaw)**

46. *S*ad is the day for any man when he becomes absolutely satisfied with the *life* he is living, the thoughts he is thinking, and the deeds he is doing; when there ceases to be forever beating at the doors of his soul a desire to do something larger which he seeks and knows he was meant and intended to do. **(Phillips Brooks)**

47. *T*o be what we are, and to become what we are capable of becoming, is the only end of *life*.
**(Robert Louis Stevenson)**

48. *T*he shaping of our *life* is our own work; it is a thing of beauty, or a thing of shame, as we ourselves make it. We lay the corner and add joint to joint, we give the proportion, we set the finish. It may be a thing of beauty and of joy forever. God, forgive us if we pervert our *life* from putting on its appointed glory! **(William Ware)**

49. *W*e are here to add what we can to *life*, not to get what we can from *life*. **(William Osler)**

50. *Y*our purpose is an integral part of you.
(***Myles Munroe***)

51. *Y*ou are the story teller of your own *life*, and you can create your own legend, or not.
(***Isabel Allende***)

52. *W*e're not primarily put on this earth to see through one another, but to see one another through.
(***Peter De Vries***)

53. *T*here was never yet an uninteresting *life*. Such a thing is impossibility. Inside of the dullest exterior, there is a drama, a comedy and a tragedy.
(***Mark Twain***)

54. *Life* is just a chance to grow a soul.
(***A. Powell Davies***)

55. *J*ust go to the mirror and look at yourself
And see what the man has to say;
For it isn't your father, or mother, or wife,
Who, judgment upon you must pass.
The fellow whose verdict counts most in your *life*,
Is the one starring back from the glass.     (*********)

56. *S*o, get busy on yourself. You are the one person for whom you are entirely responsible. Your world, your *life* can be better only if you make it so. As you improve yourself, you influence all others around you. Keep in mind that you came into this *life* with a purpose to perform. (***Harold Sherman***)

57. **H**ere is the test to find whether your mission on earth is finished: If you're alive, it isn't.

**(Richard Bach)**

58. **L**ord, maker of desires and dreams, hold me close to the heart of thy spirit so that by the grace of thy almighty hand, I will be able to fulfill the reason you placed me here on this earth by following and accomplishing my dreams.

**(Conway Stone)**

# CHAPTER TWENTY
## LIFE IS *"A BOOK / A SCHOOL"*

**L**ife is a book, in three volumes: the past, the present and the yet to be; the first is finished and laid aside; the second, we are reading day by day; the third and last of the volumes is locked from sight; God keeps the key.

*(***)*

2. *I* think of *life* as a good book. The further you get into it, the more it begins to make sense.

*(Harold S. Kushner)*

3.  *If* you want your ***life*** to be a magnificent story, then begin by realizing that you are the author and every day you have the opportunity to write a new page. **(Mark Houlahan)**

4.  ***Life*** is a leaf of paper white

    Whereon each one of us may write

    His word or two, and then comes night.

    Greatly begin! Though thou have time

    But for a line, be that sublime –

    Not failure, but low aim, is crime.

    **(James Russell Lowell)**

5.  *T*he human race may be compared to a writer. At the outset, a writer has often only a vague general notion of the plan of his work, and of the thought he intends to elaborate. As he proceeds, penetrating his material, laboring to express himself fitly, he lays a firmer grasp on his thought; he finds himself. So, the human race is writing its story, finding itself, discovering its own underlying purpose, revising, recasting a tale pathetic often, yet none the less sublime. **(Felix Adler)**

6.  *E*very day is an opportunity to be creative - the canvas is your mind, the brushes and colours are your thoughts and feelings, the panorama is your story, the complete picture is a work of art called, 'my ***life***'. Be careful what you put on the canvas of your mind today - it matters. **(Inner Space)**

7.  *T*he *life* of every man is a diary in which he means to write one story, and writes another, and his humblest hour is when he compares the volume as it is with what he vowed to make it.

    **(James M. Barrie)**

8.  *Y*our *life* is like a book. The title page is your name; the preface, your introduction to the world. The pages are a daily record of your efforts, trials, pleasures, and discouragements. Day by day, your thoughts and acts are being inscribed in your book of *life*. Hour by hour, the record is being made that must stand for all time. One day the word *'finis'* must be written. Let it then be said of your book that it is a record of noble purpose, generous service and work well done.     **(Grenville Kleiser)**

9.  *L*ife is like a book. Your story does not end because of one bad chapter in your life. Some chapters are sad, some happy, and some exciting. But if you never turn the page, you will never know what the next chapter holds. Keep going! Don't give up!     **(***)**

10. *Y*ou are writing a gospel, a chapter each day, by the deeds that you do, and the words that you say. Men read what you write, if it's false or is true. Now what is the gospel according to you?     **(***)**

11. **L**ife is God's novel. Let Him write it.

    **(Isaac Bashevis Singer)**

12. **Life** resembles a novel more often than novels resemble **life**.     **(George Sand)**

13  *T*he world is a book where those who do not take risks read only one page.  **(John Mason)**

14. *N*ature is man's religious book, with lessons for every day.  **(Theodore Parker)**

15. *My life* is my message.  **(Mahatma Ghandi)**

16. *T*he course of *life* is unpredictable… no one can write his autobiography in advance.
**(Abraham Joshua Heschel)**

17. *T*he whole of *life* is a stage and the mighty play goes on so you can add a verse. What will your verse be?  **(Shakespeare)**

18. **Life** is a great school in which you are constantly learning how better to work, plan and achieve. The schoolmaster of *life* may be seen stern and relentless, but the discipline is for your ultimate good.  **(Grenville Kleiser)**

19. **Life** is the toughest school. You never know what class you are in, what exam you will have next and you can't cheat because nobody else has the same question paper. Many people fail because they try to copy others, not realizing that everyone has a different question paper.  **(***)**

20. *E*xample is the school of mankind and they will learn at no other.  **(Edmund Burke)**

21. **Life** is my college. May I graduate well, and earn some honours!  **(Louisa May Alcott)**

22. **H**ard times have a way of teaching us lessons that we refuse to learn in good times. That is the one university we all get to attend - tuition free.

**(Clarence Thomas)**

23. **Life** is like one long university education where you can learn more every day. **(***)**

24. **T**he world is a great university. From the cradle to the grave we are always in God's great kindergarten, where everything is trying to teach us a lesson. **(Orison Swett Marden)**

25. **Life** is a mystery to be lived and not a problem to be solved. **(***)**

# CONCLUSION

*Life* is a struggle; face it!

*Life* is a journey; complete it!

*Life* is taking risks; dare them!

*Life* is seizing opportunities; make the most of them!

*Life* is courageousness; never be scared!

*Life* is determination; run until you break the tape!

*Life* is striking at a balance; live within your possibilities!

*Life* is time; leave nothing to chance!

*Life* is the past, present, and the future; **now** is the watchword!

*Life* is beyond birth and death; endure cheerfully the trials which come to you!

*Life* is a virtue; watch the way you live!

*Life* is concern for others; give and make sacrifices!

*Life* is trusting in God; have faith!

**Life** is cheerfulness; learn to smile and laugh!

**Life** is enjoying friendship; consolidate the joy!

**Life** is enjoying recreation; it is an imperative!

**Life** is enjoying little acts; do them nobly!

**Life** is following rules; if you break them, they will break you!

**Life** is a purpose; recognize it and be used up!

**Life** is a book; you are the author! Engrave, in it, your autobiography in gold!

**Life** is a school; learn your lessons and graduate with honours!

# NAME INDEX

www.ingramcontent.com/pod-product-compliance
Lightning Source LLC
Chambersburg PA
CBHW031123250726

48655CB00004B/1824